STUDENT ENGAGEMENT IN THE DIGITAL UNIVERSITY

Student Engagement in the Digital University challenges mainstream conceptions and assumptions about students' engagement with digital resources in Higher Education. While engagement in online learning environments is often reduced to sets of transferable skills or typological categories, the authors propose that these experiences must be understood as embodied, socially situated, and taking place in complex networks of human and nonhuman actors. Using empirical data from a JISC-funded project on digital literacies, this book performs a sociomaterial analysis of student–technology interactions, complicating the optimistic and utopian narratives surrounding technology and education today and positing far-reaching implications for research, policy and practice.

Lesley Gourlay is Head of the Department of Culture, Communication and Media and Reader in Education and Technology at the Institute of Education, University College London, UK. She is Co-Convener of the Society for Research into Higher Education's UK-wide Digital University Network, and Executive Editor for the journal *Teaching in Higher Education*.

Martin Oliver is Professor of Education and Technology and Head of the Centre for Doctoral Education at the Institute of Education, University College London, UK. He has edited the journals *Research in Learning Technology* and *Learning, Media and Technology*, and is Past President of the Association for Learning Technology.

STUDENT ENGAGEMENT IN THE DIGITAL UNIVERSITY

Sociomaterial Assemblages

Lesley Gourlay and Martin Oliver

Routledge
Taylor & Francis Group

NEW YORK AND LONDON

First published 2018
by Routledge
711 Third Avenue, New York, NY 10017

and by Routledge
2 Park Square, Milton Park, Abingdon, Oxon, OX14 4RN

Routledge is an imprint of the Taylor & Francis Group, an Informa business

Library of Congress Cataloging-in-Publication Data
A catalog record for this book has been requested

ISBN: 978-1-138-12538-4 (hbk)
ISBN: 978-1-138-12539-1 (pbk)
ISBN: 978-1-315-64752-4 (ebk)

Typeset in Bembo
by Sunrise Setting Ltd., Brixham, UK

CONTENTS

ACKNOWLEDGEMENTS

We would like to thank JISC for their generous support in funding the project described in this book and also for their tolerance on the several occasions we may have strayed from our original brief. Their flexibility allowed us the space to develop our ideas in conversation with the other project teams, while their practical and developmental focus always reminded us that it was incumbent on us not merely to critique the status quo, but also to try to make a difference to educational practice. We also thank the Institute of Education (IOE) for hosting the study and providing us with robust support throughout. We are grateful to Jude Fransman for her insightful input on the methodological design and her sensitive data collection on the project. Wilma Clarke did a meticulous job of processing the interview data in NVIVO. Susan McGrath supported the recruitment of participants via the student union and helped organise the focus groups. Lindsay Jordan's creativity and insight as an educational developer allowed the data to be converted to workshop materials for staff and students. She was supported in this by the UK Staff and Educational Development Association (SEDA). Nazlin Bhimani and Barbara Sakarya of the IOE Library, in consultation with the UK Society of College, National and University Libraries (SCONUL), created engaging and thoughtful resources for staff via the LibGuide, also based on the project findings. Stephen Hill led an innovative online synchronous offer for the students in the Academic Writing Centre and followed it up with a focus group – thanks too for his contribution. Thanks also to the UK Association of Learning Technologists (ALT) for hosting a webinar with Mary Hamilton, partly derived from the project findings, and to the journal *Research in Learning Technology* for the opportunity to contribute to a special issue on this topic. Throughout the publication of various associated papers and the development of this book, we have benefitted from a series of ongoing conversations and insights gained from anonymous journal reviewers and from the work of associates across our field. These include Mary Lea, Robin Goodfellow, Mary Hamilton, Norm Friesen, Tara Fenwick, Richard Edwards, Chris Jones, Sian Bayne, Jen Ross, Jeremy Knox, Ibrar Bhatt, Donna Lanclos and many more. We are also grateful to Alex Masulis and Dan Schwartz at Routledge New York for their endless patience and understanding, while we at times struggled to find time in busy academic lives for the *assemblage* that has resulted in this book to emerge and thrive – it happened somewhat more gradually than originally intended. Thanks to them for believing in the project.

Several of the chapters develop and seek to deepen and interrelate themes from papers published elsewhere. Chapter 1 extends the discussion on student engagement in Gourlay, L. 2015. 'Student engagement and the tyranny of participation', published in *Teaching in Higher Education* 20(4), 402–411. Chapter 2 develops some points first made in Gourlay, L. 2015. 'Open education as a heterotopia of desire', published in *Learning, Media and Technology*. Chapter 7 draws on some points made in the joint paper Gourlay, L., Hamilton, M. and Lea, M. 2013. 'Textual practices in the new media landscape: messing with digital literacies', published in *Research in Learning Technology* (21). The visual methodology used in the project and described in Chapter 5 was discussed in Gourlay, L. 2010. 'Multimodality, visual methodologies and higher education', In Savin-Baden, M. and Howell Major, C. (Eds.), *New Approaches to Qualitative Research: Wisdom and Uncertainty*. London: Routledge, 80–88., and also in Gourlay and Oliver 2015. 'Multimodal longitudinal journaling', in Haythornthwaite, C., Andrews, R., Fransman, J. and Kazman, M. *The SAGE Handbook of Elearning Research* (2nd Ed.), London, SAGE. Chapter 7 develops an earlier analysis in Gourlay and Oliver 2016, *It's not all about the learner: a sociomaterial reframing of students' digital literacy practices*. In Ryberg, T., Bayne, S., Sinclair, C. and de Laat, M. (Eds.) Research, Boundaries, and Policy in Networked Learning. London: Routledge, 77–92. Chapter 8 examines and relates data discussed separately in Gourlay, L. and Oliver, M. 2015. 'Students' physical and digital sites of study: making, marking and breaking boundaries', in Carvalho, L., Goodyear, P. and de Laat, M. (Eds.) *Place-Based Spaces for Networked Learning*, London: Routledge, and in Gourlay, L. 2014. 'Creating time: students, technologies and temporal practices in higher education', published in *E-Learning and Digital Media*, 11(2), 141–153. The ideas on staff development are based on Gourlay and Oliver 2016. 'Reflecting on things: sociomaterial perspectives on academic development', published in Leibowitz, B., Bozalek, and Kahn, P. *Theorising Professional Development for Teaching in Higher Education*, London: Society for Research into Higher Education, Routledge. This book has allowed us the opportunity to draw together, move forward and relate together the ideas from these earlier publications.

Thanks also to UCL IOE for the sabbatical time we were granted to devote to this, and particularly to departmental administrator Fran Reubens, who has managed diaries and protected precious writing time when it was most urgently needed. Most importantly, we would like to thank the student participants in this study for their time, their sometimes penetrating insights, their commitment, and the privilege of being able to glimpse their engagement and unfolding entanglements in the digital university.

1

INTRODUCTION

As the influence of digital technologies becomes more pervasive throughout society and education, what it means to be a student and to engage in Higher Education is changing, often in ways which appear to overturn or transform the nature of learning and the university itself. These changes are indeed far-reaching, as the way that we communicate and access information becomes increasingly permeated with digital technologies. We use mobile networked devices to interact with technologies and online platforms while on the move, which has radically altered how we lead our lives, including in educational settings. Social media use has blurred the boundaries between private and public and has opened up new opportunities to explore and create multiple ways of being online. Meanwhile, the sheer volume of online information has expanded the range of texts and resources available to students, enhancing their educational opportunities, but also presenting them – and the university – with fresh challenges.

However, there has been a tendency in popular culture and in educational circles to regard the influence of the digital as a revolutionary change unlike any other, one which will entirely sweep away previous practices and fundamentally alter all aspects of scholarship and the quest for knowledge. This is sometimes related to assumed absolute generational differences, with notions like the 'digital native' (Prensky 2001) becoming popularised in the mainstream media. We have also seen the rise of the notion that all pre-digital practices are inherently retrograde and should be replaced by (supposedly superior) digital technologies. These ideas, we argue, stem from a tendency to enrol digital technologies as a signifier of other ideas and values related to education – such as notions of freedom, speed and efficiency – which seductively give the impression that the digital can allow us to transcend the limits of the body and our social and material settings, or do away completely with notions of expertise or the need for teachers and so-called traditional modes of scholarship.

This book examines how the digital is discussed and used in Higher Education and looks in particular at how these discourses and ideologies position students, lecturers, scholarship, knowledge and ultimately the university itself. We argue for a need to focus on what students actually *do* day-to-day in their independent study time, drawing on a research project which investigated the practices and perspectives of a small number of postgraduate students over the period of a year. In doing so, we argue for a 'resituating' of how we theorise student engagement in the digital university, moving away from categories, abstractions, fantasies and ideologies, and towards a *sociomaterial* understanding of this as embodied practice.

This chapter will identify the main themes of the book, setting these within the broader context of developments in contemporary Higher Education, and will give an overview of the book's structure. In considering this complex topic, we will begin by critically examining two key concepts often used in Higher Education to talk about students, and we will also examine concepts and terms often used in relation to digital technologies.

'The Student Experience'

Contemporary policies in Higher Education across the world have followed a similar pattern, with an increasing focus on 'the student experience'. This concept has become central to discussions of educational quality, and has contributed to comparisons that form the basis of league tables, nationally and internationally (Barefoot *et al.* 2016). This move arguably forms part of a long-term change in the relationship between Higher Education and society, a relationship in which universities are increasingly expected to operate as if they were in a market and less as a form of public good. In the UK, students began to be identified as customers from the time of the government-commissioned Dearing report onwards (Dearing 1997). The rhetoric of UK national policy more recently has been to place 'students at the heart of the system' (Department for Business, Innovation and Skills (BIS) 2011), positioning them as informed consumers within a competitive Higher Education marketplace. Linked to this are the league tables, drawing on data from national surveys of student satisfaction, such as the National Survey of Student Engagement in the US, the National Student Survey in the UK and the Australasian Survey of Student Engagement (Richardson 2005).

Alongside this development, debates about the purposes of Higher Education are taking place; discussions about the relationship between Higher Education and industry in particular have been going on for over a century, and have arisen wherever there are universities (Taylor 1999). In recent years, however, this discussion has focused particularly on ensuring the supply of appropriately trained graduates. In the UK, Higher Education has increasingly been repositioned as a private investment made by an individual, one expected to pay off in terms of subsequent earnings, and the system as a whole has been positioned as a driver for industrial innovation and the economy. In the US, the American Association of

State Colleges and Universities identified the growth of online learning as one of its top ten priorities for 2013 – the top position being held by the need for public colleges and universities to achieve state goals through 'overall degree production' (AASCU State Relations and Policy Analysis Team 2013). In Europe, the European Commission's 'Opening up Education' agenda focuses on the role of Higher Education in 'boosting EU competitiveness and growth through better skilled workforce and more employment' (European Commission 2013:2), for example through students developing 'digital competencies [. . .] essential for employment' (*ibid.* 6). Universities in the UK are required to provide evidence about the employment patterns of past graduates, as if this past performance enables potential students to invest their fees more wisely (Barefoot *et al.* 2016).

The concept of the student experience has come to particular prominence in the UK in a context where tuition fees were introduced and were permitted to increase to £9,000 in 2012 following the Browne Review (Browne 2010). Additionally, as Bunce *et al.* (2016) point out, the model of student-as-consumer in the UK has been underscored by the inclusion of students under the Consumer Rights Act (2015). In this climate, student satisfaction has understandably become a priority in a situation where students are required to take on substantial loans, and a consumer identity has been shown to be associated with higher student expectations (Kandiko and Mawer 2013, Tomlinson 2017). As Ramsden has argued:

> They are more liable than earlier generations to evaluate the experience of higher education as part of the broader context of their social and business networks. They are more likely to complain if the support services they encounter are inadequate or do not compare to their equivalents outside higher education.
>
> *(Ramsden 2008:3)*

However, the criticism can be made that policies and discourses positioning the individual student-as-consumer suggest a straightforward transaction via the purchase of a definable and clearly delineated product. This seems an inappropriate metaphor to be applied to an educational process which is extended, highly complex and involves a great deal of effort on the part of the student, and the effect of constructing the student-as-consumer can lead to the student being cast as a passive recipient (e.g. Molesworth *et al.* 2009). Presented as a singular concept, it can also lead to a homogenising effect. Sabri (2011) critiques the UK government policy document *Higher Ambitions: The Future of Universities in a Knowledge Economy* (BIS 2009), in particular the chapter entitled 'The Student Experience in Higher Education', which states:

> . . . as they are the most important clients of higher education, students' own assessments of the service they receive at university should be central to

our judgement of the success of our higher education system. Their choices and expectations should play an important part in shaping the courses universities provide and in encouraging universities to adapt and improve their service.

(BIS 2009:70)

As Sabri argues in relation to this quote, this has led to a reductionism:

The 'student experience' has come to be used as a singular reified entity. 'Student' becomes an adjective describing a homogenised 'experience' undifferentiated by ethnicity, socio-economic background, age or personal history. Its use precludes questions about where and when this 'experience' stops and starts, how it comes about, and how it changes. . . . a reified 'student experience' is wielded as a criterion for judgement about what is and is not worthwhile in higher education. Contained in this quote are several demands for the exclusion of and silencing of other accounts of higher education: students are 'the most important clients' of HE, and their assessment of it as 'a service' should be central to our judgement.

(Sabri 2011:2)

Arguably, the discourse of the student experience and the related notion of student satisfaction attribute a disproportionately large degree of agency to the university, or the academics, who are constructed in this model as the active players and providers of educational experience to the student who is cast as an implicitly passive and largely non-agentive consumer. The notion of satisfaction serves to reinforce the idea of Higher Education as a singular commodity which can be judged. It also reinforces the idea that Higher Education is a clear, complete and *a priori* entity which can be identified, delineated and evaluated by the student – standing somehow outside of it – as opposed to a set of activities and practices which emerge only through the active involvement of the student in interaction with others, texts and artefacts. This point will be explored throughout this book.

Student Engagement as Performativity

Interestingly, a prominent parallel discourse has also emerged in Higher Education circles focused on student engagement. This concept underpins national student surveys in the UK, USA and Australasia (e.g. Kuh 2009, Kandiko 2008, Coates 2010), where evidence of the desired type of student engagement is seen as one of the bases of a successful Higher Education offer. The concept has been highly beneficial in relation to the enhancement of inclusion, retention and diversity in Higher Education – in particular in the US system (e.g. Barkley 2010, Dunne and Owen 2013, Quaye and Harper 2015). However, as argued elsewhere (Gourlay 2015), when the concept has been applied specifically to notions of what constitute desirable forms of 'teaching and learning', as opposed to broader engagement in university life, it underscores particular ideologies about how students (and lecturers) 'should' behave.

In her review of the area, Trowler (2010) refers to Coates' (2007) definition of student engagement, where specific instantiations of what she sees as good engagement are identified:

> active and collaborative learning;
> participation in challenging academic activities;
> formative communication with academic staff;
> involvement in enriching educational experiences; and
> feeling legitimated and supported by university learning communities.
>
> *(Coates 2007:122)*

As discussed in Gourlay (2017), there is an ongoing emphasis in this definition on observable, interactive activity, in particular *engagement with others*. Trowler (2010) contrasts this type of engagement, which she characterises as 'progressive', with traditional approaches, which are in her view overly associated with content, and are portrayed as retrograde and not productive in terms of supporting the type of student engagement described by Coates (2010).

In an earlier work, Coates (2007) also looks at student engagement in terms of a typology of student 'engagement styles' as opposed to focusing on activity types. The four-part categorisation proposes 'intense', 'collaborative', 'independent' and 'passive' as distinct. The first two are described in favourable terms, with the 'independent' style described broadly positively as follows, with a reluctance to collaborate presented as a hindrance (our emphasis):

> An independent style of engagement is characterised by a more academically and less socially orientated approach to study . . . Students reporting an independent style of study see themselves as participants in a supportive learning community. They see staff as being approachable, as responsive to student needs, and as encouraging and legitimating student reflection, and feedback. *These students tend to be less likely, however, to work collaboratively with other students within or beyond class, or to be involved in enriching events and activities around campus.*
>
> *(Coates 2007:133–134)*

The fourth engagement style of 'passive' is presented as problematic by Coates:

> It is likely that students whose response styles indicate passive styles of engagement rarely participate in the only or general activities and conditions linked to productive learning.
>
> *(Coates 2007:134)*

Coates' categories seem, at first reading, to express a common-sense view, that more active students will be more successful learners. However, it is worth noting the degree to which this categorisation reveals a strong emphasis on – and desire for – interactivity, interlocution and observable activity, and as a result, renders silence, thought, reticence and unobserved private study less valid – or even proscribed – as forms of student engagement. As MacFarlane (2017) has proposed, this has led to a performative culture which uncritically promotes 'active learning' and is overly focused on self-disclosure, driven by what he calls the 'student engagement movement'. He provides a robust critique of this tendency and argues for an urgent reclamation of the notion of 'student-centred' learning, positing that students should be regarded primarily as scholars who can choose how they wish to engage. As he puts it:

> Students should have the right to learn in ways that meet their needs and dispositions as persons. Here, I believe that the distinction often drawn between 'passive' as opposed to 'active' learning has become an over-simplified dualism that has led to the vilification of student who prefer to study in an undemonstrative manner, often on their own and in silence. Even reading, an activity traditionally core to advanced learning, has been labelled pejoratively as 'passive'. Student engagement policies and practices promote 'active' learning as an essential means of evidencing learning. Yet, relying on observation is a crude means of understanding the complexity of how students learn and engage. It further distorts patterns of student behaviour that are altered to satisfy such requirements. Performative expectations such as attending classes, showing an 'enthusiasm' for learning or demonstrating emotions such as 'empathy' through as self-reflective exercise are all non-academic achievements. They are merely behavioural demands that students are expected to conform with.
>
> *(MacFarlane 2017:xiv)*

This quote touches on one of the key issues and arguments we will make throughout this book – that a particular form of observable behaviour has come to stand in policy discourses for the only type of legitimate student engagement, and (more worryingly) has also come to stand as a proxy for learning itself. Anything outside of this narrow band of acceptable behaviour is discussed pejoratively as passivity on the part of the students and, if related directly to teaching, with 'teacher-centredness' and supposedly retrograde approaches to pedagogy. We will return to this point throughout the book when looking at what students are actually doing when engaged in silent and solitary study both online and offline. We will also return to the discourses of active and passive engagement when we look at 'learning spaces' in Chapter 8.

Digital Dreams and Occlusions

The notions of the student experience and student engagement tend to be applied to Higher Education in general, and the tendency is not to specify exactly what types of experiences or engagement they refer to. However, the implication is that they refer primarily to campus-based engagement, particularly the students' experience of and engagement with taught elements of their courses, and specifically the face-to-face classroom or lecture experience. This tends to be the focus of exhortations to enhance student engagement through increased interactivity, as we will see later in the book. Arguably, digital technology takes something of a back seat in these discourses, with the role of the digital somewhat neglected or occluded in mainstream discussions of student engagement.

However, that is not to say that the digital is ignored in discourses and discussions about contemporary Higher Education – instead it is often treated separately, as if it stands outside of normal or prototypical student engagement. There is a tendency for digital technologies to be described in somewhat hyperbolic terms, in which discussions of contemporary Higher Education frequently position digital technologies as revolutionary, creating a complete break from the past, with these technologies and their effects also routinely claimed to be qualitatively entirely different to what has come before. This is often associated with the notion of root-and-branch transformation of Higher Education resulting from digital technologies, with an emphasis on exponentially increased potential for learning, and a concomitant 'breaking free' from a range of elements, which are regarded in this perspective as constraints – the human body, cognitive limitations, the immediate social sphere, geographical space, time and so on.

Although it is undeniable that digital technologies have brought about profound change and have allowed us to radically extend the scope of communication and our access to resources, we argue that the strength and absolute nature of some of these claims indicates a kind of utopian thinking, suggesting dreams or fantasies at work which perhaps relate to other desires for transcendence and freedom from what are regarded as retrograde and limiting boundaries imposed by pre-digital educational settings and practices. Arguably, the extent and reach of these changes have been exaggerated and appropriated, leading to a situation where discourses of student digital engagement have been heavily influenced by these ideologically driven perspectives, and, as a result, continuities and relationships between the digital and non-digital (or analogue) are no longer recognised, or are regarded with suspicion. This will be discussed in greater depth in the next chapter.

Resituating Digital Engagement

As we have proposed above, arguably the two most influential concepts currently used in policy and educational circles relating to students in Higher Education – the student experience and student engagement – may be regarded as flawed in various respects. The concept of the student experience has been critiqued as overly singular, flattening and reductionist, eliding the diversity of the students in the system and their multiple and complex experiences. It also reinforces a market model of Higher Education by positioning the student as a customer or consumer.

This runs the risk of reducing the university to a commercial provider, also implying by extension that Higher Education can be regarded as either a service or a product. This can, in turn, lead to a conception of the student as a passive recipient of a singular and clearly delineated *a priori* paid commodity, as opposed to an active participant in a highly complex series of educational processes and practices.

In terms of agency, the notion of the student experience is something of a paradox. It appears (on the face of it) to empower students, and the associated policy documents purport to grant students greater influence in the sector, placing them 'at the heart of the system' (BIS 2011). As such, the term 'wears the clothes' of student-centredness. However, paradoxically, the student as an active participant seems strangely absent from the model – the framing of the concept seems to deny the student activity, agency and even the scholarship and practices required to gain a degree, positioning them instead primarily as passive recipients. The responsibility for the apparent problem to be solved is firmly situated with the universities and the academic staff, who are accused of risking failure in the mission to provide a student experience of high-enough quality and good value for money.

The mainstream concept of student engagement, in contrast, appears to focus on a perceived *lack* of student agency, particularly emphasising the need to maximise observable active and interactive behaviours in the classroom and online. Here the problem is seen as residing in students who are not exhibiting the type of behaviours identified as indicative of desirable student engagement. The problem is also situated with the universities and academic staff, who may be seen to be at fault if their pedagogic interventions do not result in or encourage this type of behaviour. This stance leads, as argued above, to a performative ideology, which positions lecturing, teaching, the provision of academic content, and even expertise itself, as retrograde and teacher-centred. This also generates a deficit model which positions reticent or quiet students as passive. Student engagement is regarded as activated by the right type of pedagogic design, activity or learning space. A further effect of the mainstream concept of student engagement is that it renders the practices of individual scholarship – essential for the development of knowledge and to produce assignments via reading, writing and thinking – as simultaneously invisible, implicitly flawed and insufficiently active.

It has to be recognised that both of these terms have come to prominence in very different contexts, the latter more clearly with the laudable intention of supporting students and seeking to understand the need for students to be motivated and to feel included, particularly those who might be disadvantaged, marginalised or at risk of non-completion of their courses. It is not our intention to criticise this broader use of the concept and the valuable associated research and development work. However, as a guiding concept theorising how we might understand the fundamental nature of learning and knowledge, we argue that it is limited in its theoretical purchase for the reasons given above. As we have seen, in parallel to these two discourses, discussions concerning the digital in Higher Education are equally abstracted. Rather like the discourse of student engagement, discourses concerning the digital are also dominated by notions which appear, on the face of it, to be radical and liberating. But, we argue that they are also underpinned by ideologies concerning what the university should be and how students and lecturers should behave. 'Digital dreams' and utopian thinking are widespread. These concern the nature of knowledge and scholarship, but also reveal desires to break free from various perceived constraints in what we will argue appears to be a fantasy of human transcendence, but is in fact a deeply humanist model of education.

The aim of this book is to propose an alternative perspective on student engagement in the digital university, one which takes as its starting point the actual day-to-day practices of students – in other words, what students actually *do* in their scholarship, reading and writing in terms of interaction with digital and analogue technologies. In particular, our aim is to move away from the abstracted and ideological thinking critiqued above concerning student engagement and the digital, instead focusing on specific, situated practice – socially, materially, spatially and temporally. We also aim to re-theorise student digital engagement in order to move away from the notion of the human as the sole fount of all agency – the fantasy of the free-floating and unbounded user of resources, devices, texts and tools in supposedly neutral spatial and temporal contexts. Instead, our intention is to reframe student digital engagement as a set of *sociomaterial practices*, which are achieved by complex *entanglements* with nonhuman devices, objects, digital and analogue texts, spaces and time, in order to create fluid *assemblages* of practice. In order to make this case, the book will present data from a qualitative, ethnographically oriented study, which looked in detail at student scholarship practices over the period of a year. However, before looking at the data, we will spend some time taking a more in-depth look at some of the ideologies and frameworks which dominate thinking in Higher Education in order to consider their effects.

Chapter 2 looks in more detail at how the digital has been conceptualised in mainstream discourses of Higher Education, in particular focusing on how digital technologies have been hyped and claimed to have the potential not only to change but also to transform Higher Education. Exploring the notion of digital dreams, as discussed above, we interrogate what we see as some of the persistent myths and fantasies in the sector, which exercise a considerable influence on research agendas, policy, allocation of resources and ultimately mainstream assumptions about students' digital engagement. We also explore the tendency for the sector to split the digital and the analogue into a binary, assuming they are separate and unrelated realms of practice. We argue that this evinces a tendency to enrol the digital in fantasies about education and the human, both positive and negative, generating abstract concepts and leading us away from a focus on practices.

Chapter 3 moves on to make a case for a reinstatement of the role and central importance of meaning-making and textual (including multimodal) practices in Higher Education. We argue that discourses of student engagement, and also mainstream ways of conceiving of and designing the Higher Education curriculum, fail to recognise the central and constitutive role of meaning-making, instead assuming that communication is a transparent medium, and continuing to operate on an abstracted and skills-based model. In that chapter, we also argue that, despite the hype, in reality the digital is often ignored and rendered somewhat invisible in accounts of the curriculum and scholarship. The effects of these parallel occlusions are discussed, concluding that they also contribute to the disconnect between how student engagement is conceptualised and actual student engagement on the ground. Chapter 4 develops this analysis by turning our attention to the concepts which have arisen in the sector, and in society more broadly, in relation to digital engagement. It begins by taking a critical look at typologies which seek to classify students in terms of their age, pointing out the pitfalls of making sweeping generalisations about a putative 'net generation', and examining the effects that these stories have. It moves on to examine specific frameworks which have arisen in the sector, frameworks which not only describe, but also – we propose – seek to advance deeply ideological and ultimately normative positions about student digital engagement, which echo some of the effects of the broader educational discourses critiqued in Chapter 1. We advance the argument in this chapter that assumptions about the supposed centrality of skills and competencies, still exert a strong influence over the sector, despite the critiques and alternative models offered by subsequent theoretical reframings, such as the perspectives of New Literacy Studies.

Having raised several criticisms of these dominant discourses and constructs, we spend the rest of the book seeking to make a case for an alternative conception of student engagement in the digital university. Chapter 5 provides the background to the research study, sets out the impetus and aims of the study, introduces the participants and outlines the methodology used, in particular why we chose to use a longitudinal journaling approach using visual methodologies. We also describe how we worked together with the research participants to allow meanings to emerge from study, and how we analysed the data. Chapter 6 proposes an alternative lens through which to look at student engagement with the digital, proposing the construct of the *orientation* to analyse examples from the student data as opposed to applying typological, fixed categories of student or activity. Chapter 7 seeks to 'resituate' student digital engagement by questioning the common-sense assumption that agency rests entirely with the student user. It uses the notion of nonhuman actors, drawing on Actor-Network Theory, making the case that practices emerge in complex *assemblages* of the human and nonhuman. We question the commonly used notion of digital devices as tools, arguing that this is an oversimplification and distortion of the central and agentive role that devices and other artefacts play in student digital engagement.

We also examine the assumption that the digital leads to disembodiment, instead exploring the pervasive importance and constitutive nature of materiality and the body in student engagement with the digital. Chapter 8 continues this process of resituating, by looking at how space and time are conventionally regarded as neutral contexts for practice. Drawing on theory from human geography and philosophy, we argue that these are in fact also agents in active and reflexive assemblages of practice. Chapter 9 looks at how the students worked with these assemblages to achieve their aims, drawing on the concept of *resilience* with reference to the messy, imperfect, contingent and improvised nature of agency in these complex entanglements and fluid assemblages. Chapter 10 moves the focus to look at the implications of this analysis on organisational change at the level of the university, looking at various metaphors that have been used to conceptualise organisations. We make a case for viewing the university itself as an *assemblage*, and discuss the ramifications of such an analysis on how we theorise and bring about change, focusing on entanglements with the institution. Chapter 11 goes on to propose the *assemblage* as an alternative lens for research and development. We discuss the implications of this shift in terms of research methodology, and we also look at some of the practice-focused outputs of the research project, and how they were used to try to provide an alternative perspective on student digital engagement for academics and other Higher Education professionals seeking to support and develop student engagement. We conclude by offering a tentative alternative to a framework-based account of student engagement, which is focused more on deepened awareness of the entangled, messy, emergent nature of these complex assemblages. In Chapter 12 we draw our conclusions, proposing a reclaiming of the term student engagement to reflect the sociomaterially situated, emergent, fluid, contingent nature of human and non-human entanglements, where the engagement actually takes place. We tackle the implications for a move beyond or away from abstracted, typological and ultimately ideological models which place the human at the front and centre of all agency and practice, and consider instead the implications of this analysis, potentially enriching connections for further theoretical development in the field, allowing us to work towards a more nuanced and complex set of insights into student engagement in the digital university.

References

AASCU State Relations and Policy Analysis Team. 2013. Top 10 Higher Education State Policy Issues for 2013. www.aascu.org/policy/publications/policy-matters/topten2013.pdf [Accessed 10 Aug 2017].

Barefoot, H., Oliver, M. and Mellar, H. 2016. Informed choice? How the United Kingdom's key information set fails to represent pedagogy to potential students. *Quality in Higher Education*, 22(1), 3–19.

Barkley, E. 2010. *Student Engagement Techniques: A Handbook for College Faculty*. San Francisco, CA: Wiley and Sons.

Browne, J. Department for Business, Innovation and Skills (BIS). 2010. Securing a Sustainable Future for Higher Education: An Independent Review of Higher Education and Student Finance. http://dera.ioe.ac.uk/11444/7/10-1208-securing-sustainable-higher-education-browne-report_Redacted.pdf [Accessed 10 Aug 2017].

Bunce, L., Baird, A. and Jones, S. 2016. The student-as-consumer approach in higher education and its effects on academic performance. *Studies in Higher Education* 1–21. http://dx.doi.org/10.1080/03075079.2015.1127908 [Accessed 10 Aug 2017].

Coates, H. 2007. A Model of Online and General Campus-Based Student Engagement. *Assessment and Evaluation in Higher Education* 32(2), 121–141.

Coates, H. 2010. Development of the Australasian Survey of Student Engagement (AUSSE). *Higher Education* 60(1), 1–17.

Dearing, R. 1997. *Higher Education in the Learning Society: Report of the National Committee of Enquiry into Higher Education.* London: Her Majesty's Stationary Office.

Department for Business, Innovation and Skills (BIS). 2009. *Higher Ambitions: The Future of Universities in a Knowledge Economy.* http://webarchive.nationalarchives.gov.uk/+/http:/www.bis.gov.uk/wp-content/uploads/publications/Higher-Ambitions.pdf [Accessed 10 Aug 2017].

Department for Business, Innovation and Skills (BIS). 2011. *Students at the Heart of the System.* London: The Stationary Office Limited. www.educationengland.org.uk/documents/pdfs/2011-white-paper-higher-ed.pdf [Accessed 10 Aug 2017].

Dunne, E. and Owen, D. 2013. *The Student Engagement Handbook: Practice in Higher Education.* Bingley: Emerald.

European Commission. 2013. *Opening up Education: Innovative Teaching and Learning for All Through New Technologies and Open Educational Resources.* Brussels: European Commission. https://ec.europa.eu/education/policy/strategic-framework/education-technology_en [Accessed 10 Aug 2017].

Gourlay, L. 2015. Student engagement and the tyranny of participation. *Teaching in Higher Education* 20(4), 402–411.

Gourlay, L. 2017. Student engagement, 'learnification' and the sociomaterial: critical perspectives on higher education policy. *Higher Education Policy* 30(1), 23–24.

Kandiko, C. 2008. Student Engagement in Two Countries: A Comparative Study Using National Survey of Student Engagement Data. *Journal of Institutional Research* 14(1), 71–86.

Kandiko, C. and Mawer, M. 2013. *Student Expectations and Perceptions of Higher Education.* London: King's Institute.

Kuh, G. 2009. The national survey of student engagement: conceptual and empirical foundations. *New Directions for Institutional Research* 141, 5–20.

MacFarlane, B. 2017. *Freedom to Learn: The Threat to Student Academic Freedom and Why it Needs to be Reclaimed.* London: Routledge.

Molesworth, M., Nixon, E. and Scullion, R. 2009. Having, being and higher education: The marketisation of the university and the transformation of the student into consumer. *Teaching in Higher Education* 14(3), 277–287.

Prensky, M. 2001. Digital natives, digital immigrants part 1. *On the Horizon* 9(5), 1–6.

Quaye, J. and Harper, J. (Eds.) 2015. *Student Engagement in Higher Education: Theoretical Perspectives and Practical Approaches for Diverse Populations* (2nd Ed.). New York: Routledge.

Ramsden, P. 2008. *The Future of Higher Education, Teaching and the Student Experience.* York: Higher Education Academy. www.heacademy.ac.uk/knowledge-hub/future-higher-education-teaching-and-student-experience [Accessed 10 Aug 2017].

Richardson, J. 2005. Instruments for obtaining student feedback: a review of the literature. *Assessment & Evaluation in Higher Education* 30(4), 387–415.

Sabri, D. 2011. What we miss when we focus on the student experience. *Discourse: Studies in the Cultural Politics of Education* 32(5), 657–667.

Taylor, P. 1999. *Making Sense of Academic Life: Academics, Universities and Change.* Buckingham: The Society for Research into Higher Education and Open University Press.

Tomlinson, M. 2017. Student perceptions of themselves as 'consumers' of higher education. *British Journal of Sociology of Education* 38(4), 450–467.

Trowler, V. 2010. *Student Engagement Literature Review.* York: Higher Education Academy. www.heacademy.ac.uk/system/files/studentengagementliteraturereview_1.pdf [Accessed 10 Aug 2017].

2

DIGITAL HYPE, MYTHS AND FANTASIES

Chapter 1 set out the limitations of some mainstream concepts and related assumptions concerning student engagement and the digital, and proposed that there is a need to develop a more nuanced theoretical perspective on what students do and how practice emerges, seeking to resituate student digital engagement not only socially, but also sociomaterially, with a broader conception of agency. In this chapter, we will look in more depth at how digital technology has been theorised in the Higher Education literature and in policy discourses.

We will begin by exploring and critiquing the ways in which digital technologies are described in Higher Education and the various ideas that have become associated with them. In doing so, we will examine two central claims made for the digital, claims which have attained the dubious status of apparent common sense. First, we will interrogate the widespread assumption that the digital is fundamentally 'transformative', and second, that it automatically brings about either wholesale enhancement or disruption. These assumptions will be critiqued, and we will propose that they are overblown and erroneously based on the notions that the digital is fundamentally separate from pre-existent analogue technologies, that it will inevitably supplant what came before and that it is inherently possessed of a power and agency which transcends its social and material contexts. Drawing on the work of the media theorist Friedrich Kittler, we will utilise the notion of the university as a 'media system' with long historical, social and epistemological roots. The chapter will then examine Kittler's analysis of the effects of changes in media over the centuries, disputing his claims concerning what he sees as absolute ruptures caused by technological change. Instead, we will argue for an analysis which retains the notion of continuities and combinations of prior and new technologies. We will propose that analogue practice is still central to this system, which has evolved over the centuries and continues to change in combination with the digital.

The Myth of 'Transformation'

Arguably, the central claim made for the use of the digital in Higher Education is that it is 'transformative', with the implication that it is inherently different from analogue technologies and related practices, which consist predominantly of print literacy practices, verbal encounters and other forms of embodied activity. This viewpoint reflects a wider perception in society that there is something fundamentally distinct about digital technologies in comparison with what came before, and that they will lead to wholesale root-and-branch change, sweeping away and entirely supplanting pre-existing analogue technologies, practices and subjectivities. This type of strong claim for transformation is prevalent in the Higher Education sector, both in the research literature on education and technology, and also in policy discourses. An example of the former can be seen in Barnes and Tynan (2007), who explicitly refer to a 'brave new world' in the title of their paper written ten years ago; the paper focuses on a fictional student of the future, imagined in 2012 as engaging with the university exclusively online, as opposed to attending the campus, which it is suggested would be replaced by a studio for the production of podcasts and videos. This narrative of a complete break from the past – in this case that the material campus and teachers would rapidly become obsolete as a result of digital technologies – is often accompanied by a declaration that the pre-existing educational strategy is dead. This can be seen with particular clarity in the associated rhetoric surrounding the lecture, which is frequently held up to be teacher-centred, retrograde and either obsolete or at least in dire need of remediation in the digital age (e.g. Folley 2009). This view arguably reaches its logical endpoint with the notion of the 'flipped classroom' (e.g. Tucker 2012). In this conception, teaching or 'instruction' is removed completely from the embodied, campus-based encounter, and instead is delivered via online video – providing an example of the tendency towards polarised reactions, which the presence of digital technology seems to encourage in some areas of educational thought and practice.

In addition to this tendency to overstate its transformative potential, the relationship between education and technology is also frequently characterised by the 'generally vacuous and enthusiastic excesses of "tech-talk"'(Selwyn 2016:ix), which have arguably come to dominate and guide policy and the deployment of resources. As Selwyn contends, the 'hype' of the digital must be taken seriously and subjected to critique. He points out the tendency to associate the use of the digital with educational 'enhancement', and, at a more heightened level, with the notion of 'transformation', tellingly with the language of software development being transposed into the educational context via terms such as 'Education 3.0', or 'rebooting' education. (It is noteworthy that in these increasingly commonplace coinages, education itself is positioned as a technology which can be rebooted.)

Selwyn reminds us that at the most extreme end of the spectrum, we see the use of the term 'revolution' being applied to discussions of the digital, with associated ideas of conflict and overturning of the established order. Examples of this tendency can be seen in recent UK policy documentation, whose rhetoric has tended towards hyperbole with the use of extreme terms such as 'avalanche' (Barber *et al.* 2013), a 'final frontier' (de Freitas 2013) or an 'invasion' featuring 'perils' (Krause and Lowe 2014) being deployed to suggest an almost apocalyptic transformation of Higher Education resulting from the use of digital technologies, in the latter two cases with reference to MOOCs (massive open online courses). It is noteworthy that MOOCs are presented by Krause and Lowe (2014) as alien, unknowable, threatening and possessed of potent and awe-inspiring qualities which set them outside of everyday contexts of practice – when in fact most MOOCs are simply highly regulated corporate educational websites consisting of videos, texts and discussion boards.

Selwyn's discussion also reminds us of the fundamentally ideological nature of dominant discourses surrounding the digital in Higher Education, which sit in contrast with the lack of robust and convincing research evidence for these claims. Instead, he suggests, these can be understood as 'evocative and aspirational stories' (2016:9). He proposes digital education as '. . . a potent space for voicing hopes and fears of what education might become in the near future' (2016:9). Viewed through this lens, the way that the digital is discussed can be understood on a more nuanced level. The digital as a 'potent space' – something both magical and fearsome – arguably pervades the way in which the sector considers and discusses its influence and place. In Higher Education policy, and in the sector mainstream, these stories abound, arguably reflecting hope – or even faith – in the transformative potential of the digital as a solution to the changing nature of society and the economy, debatably being put to work in the service of a neoliberal agenda of producing employable graduates ready for the demands of the post-industrial economy. (See Atkins 1999 for an incisive critique of the assumptions surrounding the employability agenda.)

Bayne explores the contentious issue of 'naming the complex, febrile relation of education to digital technology' (2015: 5), charting the rise and spread of the term 'Technology Enhanced Learning' (TEL) in the UK across policy and practice, where it has largely supplanted former, more neutral terms such as 'e-learning'. As she points out, TEL explicitly states the assumption that the addition of digital technology to education is 'a good thing'. Building on Kirkwood and Price (2014), she presents an insightful critique of how the term is used uncritically across the sector, arguing that:

> . . . far from being an unexceptionable and neutral term simply in need of clearer definition, in fact it carries with it a set of discursive limitations and deeply conservative assumptions which actively limit our capacity to be critical about education and its relation to technology.
>
> *(Bayne 2015:6)*

Bayne argues that these accounts serve to homogenise and 'black-box' technology, rendering into a service role the social activity of teaching and learning, but remaining '. . . bemusingly free from the influences of contemporary thought within the fields of science and technology studies and the philosophy of technology' (2015:9).

Fantasies and Utopian Thinking

However, these notions are not confined to the educational mainstream, but – we contend – can also be witnessed in the claims made for the digital by commentators seeking to challenge the Higher Education establishment. Over the last decade, the notion of 'connectivism' has come to prominence in digital education – an idea most closely associated with the work of George Siemens and Stephen Downes. Siemens (2005) proposes the concept as an alternative to cognitivism, behaviourism and constructivism, pointing out the exponential increase in the pace at which knowledge is developed, the increased tendency for individuals to move across different fields of work in their lifetimes, the increased role of informal learning, the lifelong nature of learning, the intertwined nature of the organisation and the individual, the agentive role of technology and the need to know how to find relevant information. He goes on to critique cognitivism, behaviourism and constructivism for their assumption that 'learning occurs within a person' (Siemens 2005), for their associated lack of recognition of the learning 'stored and manipulated by technology' and also for their neglect of how learning takes place within organisations. In this regard, his critique is insightful, in that he is seeking to reject a theory of learning which situates learning solely in the human, instead proposing a more distributed model which recognises the role of the nonhuman and technological, and also the importance of process. He contends that what is needed is a whole new theory, as opposed to attempts to modify foregoing frameworks to adapt to these changes, and he sets out the following as questions which need to be addressed:

- How are learning theories impacted when knowledge is no longer acquired in the linear manner?
- What adjustments need to made with learning theories when technology performs many of the cognitive operations previously performed by learners (information storage and retrieval)?
- How can we continue to stay current in a rapidly evolving information ecology?
- How do learning theories address moments where performance is needed in the absence of complete understanding?
- What is the impact of networks and complexity theories on learning?
- What is the impact of chaos as a complex pattern recognition process on learning?
- With increased recognition of interconnections in differing fields of knowledge, how are systems and ecology theories perceived in light of learning tasks?

(Siemens 2005)

He argues that personal experience alone is inadequate for the development of knowledge, instead emphasising how knowledge can be 'stored' in other people, highlighting the centrality of networks with reference to the work of Barabasi (2002), who states that: '. . . nodes always compete for connections because links represent survival in an interconnected world' (Barabasi 2002:106).

The emphasis here is clearly on maximising connections and recognition for effective learning. Siemens then defines connectivism as follows:

> Connectivism is the integration of principles explored by chaos, network, and complexity and self-organisation theories. Learning is a process that occurs within nebulous environments of shifting core elements – not entirely under the control of the individual. Learning (defined as actionable knowledge) can reside outside of ourselves (within an organization or a database), is focused on connecting specialized information sets, and the connections that enable us to learn more are more important than our current state of knowing. Connectivism is driven by the understanding that decisions are based on rapidly altering foundations. New information is continually being acquired. The ability to draw distinctions between important and unimportant information is vital. The ability to recognize when new information alters the landscape based on decisions made yesterday is also critical.
>
> *(Siemens 2005)*

It is worth focusing on his definition of learning here, which is described as 'actionable knowledge . . . focused on connecting specialized information sets'. He goes on to set out the principles of connectivism:

- Learning and knowledge rests in diversity of opinions.
- Learning is a process of connecting specialized nodes or information sources.
- Learning may reside in non-human appliances.
- Capacity to know more is more critical than what is currently known.
- Nurturing and maintaining connections is needed to facilitate continual learning.
- Ability to see connections between fields, ideas, and concepts is a core skill.
- Currency (accurate, up-to-date knowledge) is the intent of all connectivist learning activities.
- Decision-making is itself a learning process. Choosing what to learn and the meaning of incoming information is seen through the lens of a shifting reality. While there is a right answer now, it may be wrong tomorrow due to alterations in the information climate affecting the decision.

(Siemens 2005)

The emphasis is on currency, with 'information' being a key construct. He draws the following comparison:

> In a knowledge economy, the flow of information is the equivalent of the oil pipe in an industrial economy. Creating, preserving and utilizing information flow should be a key organizational activity.
>
> *(Siemens 2005)*

Here, knowledge is seen as akin to a valuable material resource that can be directed, stored and moved around as an entity which is clearly delineated, separate from those interacting with it and is regarded as *a priori*. Despite questioning the primacy of the individual earlier in the paper, Siemens then states that:

> The starting point of connectivism is the individual. Personal knowledge is comprised of a network, which feeds into organizations and institutions, which in turn feed back into the network, and then continue to provide learning to individual. This cycle of knowledge development (personal to network to organization) allows learners to remain current in their field through the connections they have formed.
>
> *(Siemens 2005)*

His paper does successfully identify the overemphasis on the human as a free-floating subject and primary site of engagement, a view we will critique throughout this book. However, his position can be criticised in several respects. First, his critique of cognitivism, constructivism and behaviourism implies that all three of these positions are equally influential in current thinking concerning learning, which in the case of behaviourism is debatable, although traces of its influence may persist. Also, he underestimates the extent to which (rightly or wrongly) interaction is already valorised in constructivism and does not consider other theoretical stances which also take into account the role of networks, such as Activity Theory (e.g. Nardi 1996) or Actor-Network Theory (e.g. Law 1992), both of which attempt to theorise the social as distributed, in the latter case also enrolling the nonhuman. These omissions serve to weaken the persuasiveness of the case as set out here, and commentators have pointed out further weaknesses in the claims made (e.g. Kop and Hill 2008). Verhagen (2006), in an incisive critique, argues that connectivism cannot be considered a learning theory, but is instead a pedagogical view on education; he also points out that there is nothing new in the claim that knowledge is stored in nonhuman appliances.

Connectivism, as discussed above, uses information as its key construct, with currency and the *process* of sourcing the most up-to-date and relevant information presented as more important than established knowledge itself. This may well be an important element of contemporary business practice – Siemens is referring to information gathering in a corporate setting, using informal means. However, this is a very different context from Higher Education, where accumulated knowledge and expertise underpin and form academic disciplines. Although currency is clearly important across all of fields of enquiry, Higher Education knowledge and scholarship are considerably more complex and cannot be reduced to high-speed acquisition of new information via informal networks alone.

Again, we would argue that in connectivism we see the urge towards a trans-formative narrative in relation to the digital – previous theoretical frameworks are rejected as entirely inadequate (with some potentially relevant ones ignored), and a completely newly minted theory is proposed. This in itself might have been of utility, but its scope is somewhat limited, and it is difficult to see how the construct could be applied in any meaningful way to Higher Education. In this example, we see how the notion of the digital as inherently transformative also underpins 'countercultural' critiques of power, in this case, power being cast as academic knowledge and expertise.

However, despite the apparent limitations of this perspective, it has been used as the basis of innovative challenges to traditional Higher Education, such as in the Open Educational Resources (OER) movement, some of whose key proponents are explicitly inspired by connectivism. Downes states that:

> At its heart, connectivism is the thesis that knowledge is distributed across a network of connections, and therefore that learning consists of the ability to construct and traverse those networks.
>
> *(Downes 2007)*

He states that knowledge is not propositional, instead that '. . . knowledge is literally the set of connections formed by actions and experience' (Downes 2007). This, as with Siemens (2005), represents an explicit rejection of accumulated knowledge as a canon, literature, data and expertise itself. Instead, knowledge is reduced to 'literally' the set of connections. He also states that knowledge:

> . . . may consist in part of linguistic structures, but it is not essentially based in linguistic structures, and the properties and constraints of linguistic structures are not the properties and constraints of connectivism.
>
> *(Downes 2007)*

Here, there seems to be an attempt to deny the centrality of meaning-making and textual or multimodal practices for knowledge. This is clearly a complex area, but the disavowal of communication (and implicitly text) without a clear statement of how knowledge is communicated in a connected online and presumably text-based system is puzzling.

Access to OERs and the creation of academic content via peer interaction is proposed as a fundamental challenge to the hierarchies and structures of power perceived to characterise the formal university system. However, as proposed in Gourlay (2015), these claims tend towards an over-simplistic binary between OERs and universities:

> Directed learning vs self-directed learning (or, instructivism or constructivism; or, formal vs informal; or, control learning vs free learning) – or to put it another way – does the education system serve the interests of the providers, or of the learners?
>
> *(Downes 2011:7)*

Here, Downes sets up a series of binaries, with the university characterised as dominated by 'directed learning' and 'instructivism'. In his view, it is 'formal' and encourages 'control learning'. OERs are presented as offering the opposite of these – 'self-directed learning' and 'constructivism'. They are claimed to be 'informal', offering an opportunity for 'free learning'. However, it is worth pausing at this point to consider what is being compared here. Throughout Downes's discussion, emphasis is placed on access to content. OERs are themselves 'resources'. On closer inspection, what is generally being referred to is access to texts or interactive opportunities. This emphasis arguably serves to flatten and simplify educational engagement to access to resources or the opportunity to create new content; engagement and learning itself, then implicitly becomes situated in the resource.

Formal education, it is claimed, renders students 'passive and disempowered' (Downes 2011:248). This is contrasted with the potential of 'edupunk' for the creation of new content by participants:

> Edupunk, and for that matter OERs, are not and should not be thought of in the context of the traditional educational model, where students are passive recipients of 'instruction' and 'support' and 'learning resources'. Rather, it is the much more active conception where students are engaged in the actual creation of those resources . . . this is exactly what corporations and institutions do *not* want edupunks and proponents of OERs to do, and they have expended a great deal of effort to ensure that this does not become the mainstream of learning, to ensure students remain passive and disempowered.
>
> *(Downes 2011:248)*

The joint creation of open online resources may well be a valuable and motivating activity. However, it appears what is being suggested is that the creation of resources outside of formal education should be regarded as a complete alternative, and that universities should be rejected wholesale on the basis of this analysis as inherently and deliberately repressive of students and their freedom to learn.

Although this position appears to place the needs of the students or participants first, Downes is not simply advocating for a more agentive role for students in education. Instead, he proposes a complete rejection of academic expertise, established canons of knowledge, disciplinarity or any form of teaching. Knowledge, learning, scholarship – all of these are seen instead as arising *sui generis* via lay interaction. The stance is radical, and as such appears to wear the clothes of criticality. However, we argue that if students are unable to interact critically with experts, data, texts or bodies of knowledge accumulated over the centuries, it is difficult to see what this form of engagement would consist of, or how it would build on or present meaningful or fundamental challenges to what has come before. It should of course be acknowledged that the OER movement contains a range of viewpoints; however, as a central and influential figure, Downes represents a view which is apparently widespread among OER proponents.

The OER movement has also been critiqued for positing the learner or participant as a free-floating agent with untrammelled access to participation (Knox 2013). It can be argued that the claims made for the movement are also based on hope, or desire (Gourlay 2015). Again, as with the mainstream fantasy of a solution to the challenges of the contemporary economy discussed above, we see the digital being called upon to perform some kind of alchemy – to provide solutions, and radically empower individuals to cut a swathe through what are in reality highly complex and challenging networks of practice and power, in educational contexts and beyond. Exploring the notion of the digital as a form of magic, we can also discern an opposing set of stories – those reflecting fears. In society more broadly, this can be seen in the persistent fear of human agency being lost to the digital; this may refer to very understandable worries of job losses in the face of technological development, but may also be expressed in more apocalyptic terms, centred on possible dystopian futures such as those characterised by a takeover of society by robots or computers. In relation to education and popular culture, concerns have also been raised that digital technologies are leading to a dumbing down of engagement with ideas and information (e.g. Carr 2011).

This tension – between utopian hopes for transformation and revolution, and dystopian fears of loss of control – can be seen to be interlaced in a complex web across the way we have come to talk about the digital in Higher Education (and beyond). Although apparently contradictory, they can be seen to share key attributes. As argued above, they appear to imbue the digital with extensive transformative potential, which may lead to powerfully positive or negative outcomes. As such, the digital has become a focus and repository for somewhat abstract and value-laden ideologies about the role of Higher Education in society, both conservative and more radical. In each case, ideologies concerning the human subject are also expressed – fantasies of the graduate as efficient and compliant worker in the knowledge economy, of the maverick educational outsider challenging formal structures of power, or of the free-floating autonomous human subject, untethered to social context or physical space. As we have also seen, deep fears about loss of human agency or expertise also find their expression in these notions. It is perhaps inevitable that the digital has become a repository for this complex of hopes and fears in education and beyond. However, if left unchallenged, this can take – and arguably has already taken – on the status of common-sense fact, and as such has been used to shape policy and practice in far-reaching ways.

The Dominance of 'Digital Dualism'

The digital, however apparently dazzling and different, does not reside in a separate and magical realm outside of our social and material world, but instead exists in complex continuities and entanglements with the social, the embodied, the material and the analogue. In the rest of this chapter, we will argue for a more nuanced viewpoint which seeks to question what Jurgensen (2011) calls 'digital dualism' – the tendency to posit the analogue and the digital as a clearly observable binary. A feature which characterises this dualism is the tendency to present the digital alone as technology, implicitly excluding the non-digital from that category. As a result, the technological status of print-based practices and artefacts is rendered invisible, arguably leading to a view that these come to be seen as 'given' elements of education, which is portrayed as an entity standing somehow outside of technology. As argued elsewhere (e.g. Gourlay 2012), the analogue technologies of inscription and communication in Higher Education have become naturalised to the point of invisibility, while the novelty of the digital has led to it being reified as prototypically technological.

The German media theorist Friedrich Kittler argued persuasively in his detailed historical analysis that the university can be regarded as a 'media system' (Kittler 2004), which has undergone successive changes surrounding media and technology over the centuries, changes such as the introduction of the printing press. These changes have also led in the past to profound changes (but also continuities) in how education was conducted, in terms of day-to-day practices as well as in the ways in which knowledge was constructed, communicated and disseminated. As Freisen and Cresswell point out in their insightful discussion of Kittler:

> The strident positions of both the critics and enthusiasts in these debates ignore the historical imbrication of education and media, as well as the fact that media are not reducible to their content just as education is not reducible to its curricula. The university – among the oldest continuously operating institutions, east or west – has developed to its contemporary form in intimate interrelationship with the emergence of various mediatic technology for storing, producing and disseminating knowledge.
>
> *(Freisen and Cresswell 2010:1)*

Kittler's analysis provides us with a means by which to recognise the constitutive role of the media in the university, as Freisen and Cresswell elaborate in their analysis of the relationship between media and pedagogy. It can be argued that Kittler's view of technology reflects a somewhat polemical and deterministic stance, in which technological change is regarded as a catalyst for absolute rupture from preceding mediatic conditions, rather like the scorched earth pronouncements of connectivism. However, as Winthrop-Young observes, '. . . Kittler is too good a historian to seriously believe in immaculate media conception. New media do not drop unannounced out of the sky like meteoroids or extraterrestrial Transformers' (Winthrop-Young 2010:64–65). As Winthrop-Young points out, Kittler's antipathy to economic, sociological or humanistic explanations of mediatic change leads him to posit '. . . an autonomous media-technological evolution driven by an internal dynamic' in which 'humans are at best along for the ride' (Winthrop-Young 2010:65). In Kittler's later analyses of digital technology he goes a step further, casting software in particular as doing no more than conjuring an illusion of human agency, 'a postmodern Tower of Babel' (Kittler 1997:148), designed to dupe the user and conceal its true nature. Change is seen as inevitable, apocalyptic and one-way; '. . . number series, blueprints, and diagrams never turn back into writing, only into machines' (Kittler 1999:xl).

Here, arguably, we see the viewpoints critiqued above being underscored, with reference to media technology in general, in a strongly deterministic model in which human agency is not only threatened but also obviated. As we have seen, in mainstream educational discourses, there is a tendency towards a belief that new technology – in particular the digital – will inevitably sweep away all that has preceded it. This view is present in two apparently different views of agency: one in which the human is seen as an all-powerful user of tools, in this case the assumption is that all prior technology will be replaced as retrograde; or one in which agency is seen to reside entirely in technology, with the human relegated to a helpless pawn, powerless in the face of the relentless march of technological progress. These two opposing assumptions surrounding agency have come to permeate educational thought.

However, one feature of these various accounts is the lack of research evidence into the detail of day-to-day practices in educational settings. In TEL research, the focus is all too often on an attempt to prove the efficacy of a particular digital intervention and is often conducted by enthusiasts who may already be convinced of the inherent superiority of a particular piece of technology over what preceded it. It is also dominated by research into online engagement in isolation, with less focus having been placed on how this engagement combined with the complex web of meaning-making practices at work in Higher Education; it also neglects to focus on how the digital is used day-to-day on campus and beyond in everyday scholarship.

However, a cursory reflection on one's own practices as an academic, and those observed in students, immediately starts to undermine the assumption. Throughout daily life, and in particular when engaged in scholarship, the digital is used in combination with print literacy artefacts such as books, paper and pens, highlighters and so on. Texts are transformed and merged, made up of a mixture of handwritten notes, Post-its, notes on phones and digital texts. There is no meaningful separation between digital and analogue practice in the sense that they are constantly intertwined and acting on one another at the level of engagement. Texts are printed and also scanned – they therefore frequently cross between a digital and analogue status. This accords with Levy's (2003) discussion of the status of the document in the contemporary library, in which he challenges the notion of the digital document as fluid and the analogue document as fixed. Instead, he argues for a conception of digital and analogue texts as constantly in circulation. Chapter 3 will return to the theme of the nature of texts in the digital university in more detail, but for now the key point is that the apparent eradication of print literacy artefacts and practices by their digital successors does not seem to have taken place.

Conclusions

In this chapter, we have looked at the ways in which digital technologies are discussed in Higher Education, looking first at somewhat overstated and utopian conceptions of the digital revolutionising the system and supplanting all that came before, unleashing a transcendent new set of potentials for the human – who nonetheless remains at the centre of the model, despite the claims made for the power and transformative potential of technologies. We have also examined the claims made by commentators seeking to re-theorise digital engagement with an emphasis on networks and distributed agency, arguing that this stance, although insightful in many regards, effectively 'throws the baby out with the bathwater' with its narrow definition of knowledge and wholesale rejection of all foregoing scholarship and expertise. We have also sought to undermine the assumption that the digital resides in a separate and rarefied realm, removed from the material and the analogue in terms of artefacts and practices. It is undeniable that increased digitisation of the university has led to radical changes in what it means to be a student. We can observe significant shifts in how students engage in day-to-day activities and tasks, with the practices and spaces conventionally associated with campus-based engagement increasingly permeated with digital devices and media working in networks alongside persistent print-based artefacts and technologies. However, engagement in the contemporary university is also intermeshed with traditional media alongside digitisation.

This observation provides a challenge to the somewhat dramatic revolution narratives discussed above, providing an alternative starting point, which might allow us to discern continuities and assemblages of resources, as opposed to sub-scribing to an absolutist scorched earth conception of digital revolution and rupture. Instead, we propose that contemporary Higher Education has adopted new digital technologies in a manner which – although clearly leading to profound change – is also intertwined with existing analogue technologies, always in an embodied and particular setting, which may be the physical environment of the campus or a range of other settings. In this regard, these embodied practices should also be seen as part of what constitutes the digital university, undermining 'digital dualisms' that propose a radical break between old and new visions of Higher Education. We will return to this theme in subsequent chapters, illustrating this point with data from our study, which focused on individual private study prac-tices, access and engagement with reading materials, library use and academic writing. However, we will first turn our attention to what we see as two occlusions in mainstream thought concerning student engagement in the digital university – the centrality of meaning-making and the often-neglected and less obvious pervasive entangling of the digital throughout educational processes.

References

Atkins, M. 1999. Oven-ready and self-basting: taking stock of employability skills. *Teaching in Higher Education* 4(2), 267–280.

Barabasi, A. 2002. *Linked: The New Science of Networks.* Cambridge, MA: Perseus Publishing.

Barber, M., Donnelly, K., Rizvi, S. and Summers, L. 2013. *An Avalanche Is Coming.* London: Institute for Public Policy Research. www.ippr.org/publication/55/10432/an-avalanche-iscoming-higher-education-and-the-revolution-ahead [Accessed 10 Aug 2017].

Barnes, C. and Tynan, B. 2007. The adventures of Miranda in the brave new world: learning in a Web 2.0 millennium. *ALT-J, Research in Learning Technology* 15(3), 189–200.

Bayne, S. 2015. What's the matter with 'technology-enhanced learning'? *Learning, Media and Technology* 40(1), 5–20.

Carr, N. 2011. *The Shallows: How the Internet is Changing the Way We Think, Read and Remember.* New York: Norton.

de Freitas, S. 2013. *MOOCs: The final frontier for higher education.* Coventry: Coventry University. http://researchrepository.murdoch.edu.au/id/eprint/28971/1/MOOCS_report.pdf. [Accessed 10 Aug 2017].

Downes, S. 2007. *What Connectivism Is.* http://halfanhour.blogspot.co.uk/2007/02/what-connectivism-is.html [Accessed 26 Jul 2017].

Downes, S. 2011. *Free Learning: Essays on Open Educational and Copyright.* www.downes.ca/files/FreeLearning.pdf [Accessed 11 Jul 2017].

Folley, D. 2009. The lecture is dead long live the e-lecture. In *The Proceedings of the 8th European Conference on E-Learning* (pp. 204–211). Italy: University of Bari.

Freisen, N. and Cresswell, D. 2010. Media theory, education and the university: a response to Kittler's history of the university as a media system. *Canadian Journal of Media Studies* 7(1).

Gourlay, L. 2012. Cyborg ontologies and the lecturer's voice: a posthuman reading of the 'face-to-face'. *Learning, Media and Technology* 37(2), 198–211.

Gourlay, L. 2015. Open education as a heterotopia of desire. *Learning, Media and Technology* 40(3), 310–327.

Jurgensen, N. 2011. Digital dualism versus augmented reality. *Cyborgology* https://thesocietypages.org/cyborgology/2011/02/24/digital-dualism-versus-augmented-reality/ [Accessed 11 Jul 2017].

Kirkwood, A. and Price, L. 2014. Technology-enhanced learning and teaching in higher education: what is 'enhanced' and how do we know? A critical literature review. *Learning, Media and Technology* 39(1), 6–36.

Kittler, F. 1997. *Literature Media Information Systems.* Amsterdam: John Johnston.

Kittler, F. 1999. *Gramophone, Film, Typewriter.* Trans. and intro G. Winthrop-Young and M. Wutz. Stanford, CA: Stanford University Press.

Kittler, F. 2004. Universities: wet, hard, soft and harder. *Critical Enquiry* 31(1), 244–256.

Knox, J. 2013. Five critiques of the open educational resources movement. *Teaching in Higher Education* 18(8), 821–832.

Kop, R. and Hill, A. 2008. Connectivism: learning theory of the future or vestige of the past? *The International Review of Research in Open and Distributed Learning* 9(3).

Krause, S. and Lowe, C. 2014. *Invasion of the MOOCs: The Promises and Perils of Massive Open Online Courses.* Anderson, SC: Parlor Press. www.parlorpress.com/pdf/invasion_of_the_moocs.pdf [Accessed 10 Aug 2017].

Law, J. 1992. Notes on the theory of the actor-network: ordering, strategy, and hetero-geneity. *Systemic Practice and Action Research* 5(4), 379–393.

Levy, D. 2003. Documents and libraries: a sociotechnical perspective. In A. Peterson Bishop, N. Van House and B. Buttenfield (Eds.), *Digital Library Use: Social Practice in Design and Evaluation*. Cambridge, MA: MIT Press, 25–42.

Nardi, B. 1996. *Context and Consciousness: Activity Theory and Human–Computer Interaction.* Cambridge, MA: MIT Press.

Selwyn, N. 2016. *Is Technology Good for Education?* Cambridge: Polity.

Siemens, G. 2005. Connectivism: a learning theory for the digital age. *International Journal of Instructional Technology and Distance Learning* 2(1), 3–10. www.itdl.org/Journal/Jan_05/article01.htm [Accessed 10 Aug 2017].

Tucker, B. 2012. The flipped classroom: online instruction at home frees class time for learning. *Education Next* 12(1), 82–83. http://educationnext.org/the-flipped-classroom/ [Accessed 10 Aug 2017].

Verhagen, P. 2006. *Connectivism: A new learning theory?* Surf e-learning themasite. www.surfspace.nl/nl/Redactieomgeving/Publicaties/Documents/Connectivism%20a%20new%20theory.pdf [Accessed 10 Aug 2017].

Winthrop-Young, G. 2010. *Kittler and the Media.* Cambridge: Polity Press.

3

HIDDEN TEXTS AND THE DIGITAL INVISIBLE

In Chapter 2, we questioned the tendency to imbue the digital with untold potency, in either utopian or dystopian framings, and also challenged the notion that the digital can be clearly separated from the analogue in practice. This chapter will take this reframing and resituating of student engagement in the digital university a step further, arguing that the fundamentally meaning-making and textual (including multimodal) nature of educational engagement and scholarship has been overlooked in the mainstream literature and also in the literature concerned with the digital. We will also argue, conversely, that the permeation of the digital has been overlooked in mainstream accounts of the curriculum and student engagement.

Hidden Meaning-making

Mainstream definitions of digital engagement – or more commonly, 'digital literacies' – range from a focus on activities, qualities or attributes of the student, to the practice itself. The term has arguably come to be used as a proxy for skills, with the increasing prevalence of the term 'digital literacy skills' evincing the powerful and persistent lure of that model. This conflation has come about partly due to the predominance of skills frameworks in education more broadly, which have become mainstream to the extent that they tend to loom large in conceptions of educational purpose and outcomes. These frameworks are explored in depth in Chapter 4, but for now we will take a step back in order to interrogate sector-level generic frameworks, using them to account for student engagement and looking in particular at one of the most influential concepts used in Higher Education to design, delineate and describe the discipline-based curriculum itself – the 'learning outcome'.

'Learning Outcomes', Performativity and Abstraction

In Higher Education, as in pre-tertiary education, the concept of the learning outcome has become central to the design, planning and development of curricula. The concept originates in educational psychology and has been of great utility in providing a means of moving beyond lists of content areas to be covered, and shifting the focus instead to the specifics of what the student should learn and be able to do, with an emphasis on a measurable outcome at the end of the stage or unit of study. In this regard, it is widely regarded as a useful and benign construct which confers a range of advantages on Higher Education, particularly clarity of purpose and comparability within and across courses and institutions. It has aided educators to ensure alignment and avoid mismatches between learning outcomes, educational activities, assessment design, assessment criteria and feedback to students. However, it might be argued that the considerable gains of this more systematic and atomised approach to the Higher Education curriculum have also brought with them some associated losses. In this chapter, we will argue that the use of learning outcomes to frame modules in Higher Education, however useful in many respects, has served to reinforce a focus on skills, with this approach tending to privilege observable and testable outcomes – what students can demonstrably do – and in doing so has served to elide the centrality of meaning-making, texts and semiotic resources.

In a foundational paper, Marton and Saljo (1976a) argue that the outcome of learning should not be solely focused on *how much* a student has learned, but *what* they have learned. Their experiment required students to read an academic text and then explain what they considered the main point of the text to be; with the finding that students' comprehension of the text varied, Marton and Saljo (1976b) then divided the response into four levels of accuracy and complexity. This influential paper provided the field with a valuable conceptual apparatus with which to differentiate learning qualitatively.

Biggs and Collis (1982) went on to develop the SOLO (Structure of Observed Learning Outcome) taxonomy, which proposes a series of qualitative levels to be associated with learning outcomes, going from 'surface learning' ('prestructural') to 'deep learning' ('extended abstract'). These levels are linked to various verbs, which describe what the student would be doing at the different levels – surface learning in this model is associated with activities such as 'define', 'find' and 'label', while deep learning is associated with activities such as 'evaluate', 'theorise' and 'argue'. This model is associated with Bloom's 'taxonomy of educational objectives' (Bloom *et al.* 1956), also a model of increasing complexity based on activity types, with upper levels characterised by verbs such as 'creating', 'evaluating' and 'analysing'.

Biggs then popularised the influential notion of 'constructive alignment' (Biggs 1996), which he explicitly associates with constructivism, stating that '. . . learners arrive at meaning by actively selecting, and cumulatively constructing, their own knowledge, both through individual and social activity' (Biggs 1996:348). Drawing on Cohen (1987) and the notion of 'instructional alignment', he argues that in order to attain the outcomes of teaching commonly stated by academics, such as 'to think like a mathematician' (Biggs 1996:350), attention must be paid to the smaller-scale objectives and design of teaching. He uses the construct 'performances of understanding' to focus on observable behaviour as evidence of learning.

The constructive alignment approach, with a focus on learning outcomes, has arguably become the mainstream curricular model in UK Higher Education and beyond – it is featured in PgCert (postgraduate certificate) courses in 'Academic Practice' for novice lecturers, and it also takes a central role in influential material intended to provide guidance for new lecturers (e.g. Ramsden 2003, Biggs 2011, Race 2014, Fry *et al.* 2015). Learning outcomes are routinely used in the sector to structure applications when seeking to validate new modules or programmes, drawing on the UK government's Quality Assurance Agency's (QAA) 'UK Quality Code for Higher Education' (QAA 2014), which provides a framework for qualifications granted by UK degree-awarding bodies. The descriptors used for the awards at different levels are expressed in terms of generic learning outcomes for that level of educational attainment, with these required to form the basis of specific discipline-based learning outcomes at institutional level, and the framework is aligned with 'The Framework for Qualifications of the European Higher Education Area' (EF-EHEA) (Bologna Working Group 2005). An example of one of these generic level descriptors is the following, for Master's degrees:

Master's degrees are awarded to students who have demonstrated:

- A systematic understanding of knowledge, and a critical awareness of current problems and/or new insights, much of which is at, or is informed by, the forefront of their academic discipline, field of study or area of professional practice
- A comprehensive understanding of techniques applicable to their own research or advanced scholarship
- Originality in the application of knowledge, together with a practical understanding of how established techniques of research and enquiry are used to create and interpret knowledge in the discipline
- Conceptual understanding which allows the student:
  - to evaluate critically current research and advanced scholarship in the discipline
  - to evaluate methodologies and develop critiques of them, and where appropriate, to propose new hypotheses.

(QAA 2014:28)

One critique of the learning outcomes approach is that in its desire to specify measurable outcomes, elements of knowledge and learning which are more subtle, ineffable and difficult to measure may be neglected in the model (e.g. Havnes and Proitz 2016). A further criticism might be that the learning outcomes approach neglects or elides the central role of meaning-making, texts and communication in the learning process and in the demonstration of learning outcomes. A learning outcome might, for example, state that a student should 'demonstrate awareness of' a particular concept, but the means by which this should be demonstrated is assumed to be transparent and unproblematic. In the majority of cases, despite increased interest in multimodal assessment approaches (e.g. Andrews and England 2012), it is likely to be demonstrated via linguistic textual means, typically in an essay or written exam. In the QAA generic descriptors set out above, a great deal of the outcomes would involve engagement with texts, and, in some cases, could not be arrived at by any other means outside of textual practices. Knowledge is of course developed in a range of non-textual ways, including through practice-based learning, fieldwork and experimentation. However, even these apparently non-textual activities are underpinned by linguistic and multimodal texts in the form of reading, lectures and reports, and much of the demonstration of attainment of these outcomes is likely to take place using written textual engagement.

However, the meaning-making and textual aspects of the engagement are not particularly foregrounded, as the outcomes are described in somewhat abstract terms. This is arguably necessary in the context of a national framework, in order that these generic outcomes can be flexible enough to be instantiated in the specifics of a range of programmes across all academic disciplines, fields of study or areas of professional practice. However, this abstraction in terms of exactly how these outcomes are to be attained and demonstrated is frequently replicated at the modular or programme level, with the specific practices required only made explicit at the level of assessment rubrics, with stated word limits and required formats. The effect is to create the impression that meaning-making and textual practices are unproblematic and transparent, and somehow sit outside of learning as a process, rather than seeing learning as a striving for meaning-making, where reading and writing (and speaking and listening) are both a site and a crucible of learning, rather than simply evidence of learning attained somehow prior to and outside of communication.

Leading on from this, it appears that there is a dearth of explicit focus on meaning-making and textual aspects of Higher Education at the heart of the system. However, the centrality of meaning-making is quite clearly a feature of all day-to-day Higher Education teaching and face-to-face engagement. The lecture, arguably the prototypical educational face-to-face encounter, is in fact profoundly textual (in a linguistic and multimodal sense) in its nature. The lecturer prepares a lecture in advance, on the basis of knowledge which will have been derived over a long period of engagement with texts via research and publication, reading, attendance of seminars where texts are discussed and through supervision and marking of student work where published texts are synthesised and new texts are created. The preparation is also governed by a series of texts concerned with the construction and enactment of the curriculum itself – the previous iterations of the module, perhaps a previous lecturer's slides and notes, the learning outcomes, emails from the programme leader, external examiner reports and so on (Lea and Steirer 2009). A range of texts are brought into play in the backroom work which is required in advance of the live delivery of a lecture. The lecturer may write notes by hand or digitally and is likely to produce digital slides consisting of linguistic text and multimodal semiotic resources such as images or diagrams. Students create more texts in the form of notes, download slides and begin to work towards assignments, and discuss the topic on a text-based online platform, weaving together these texts with those encountered through individual study and reading. In these respects, this verbal encounter and student engagement can be seen to be profoundly textual, but in a less observable manner, than the public texts of academic publication.

Scholars in New Literacy Studies (NLS) have drawn attention to the central role of meaning-making practices in Higher Education via a rich research literature, which has focused on student writing through the lens of academic literacies (e.g. Lea 1998, Lea and Street 1998, Ivanic 1998, Lillis 2001, Lillis *et al.* 2015, Wingate 2006). Additionally, extensive work on multimodality has allowed us to expand what we consider to be a text to include non-linguistic semiotic resources such as images, video and artefacts (e.g. Jewitt 2009, Kress 2009). However, it seems fair to say that these insights have not been picked up and incorporated by the mainstream policymakers working in quality enhancement, or in educational development – which, as discussed above, has tended to focus on a more abstracted focus on student learning, discussed in terms of either cognitive or skill-based outcomes. Commentators and scholars with an academic literacies orientation have sought to make meaning-making practices a more centrally recognised element of the mainstream university curriculum in an attempt to move away from a remedial 'deficit' model, an example of which can be seen in the 'Writing Across the Curriculum' (WAC) approach, which seeks to embed the development of academic literacies in university teaching (e.g. Bazerman *et al.* 2005). However, in the educational mainstream, meaning-making and its complex, co-constitutive and entangled relationship with knowledge, disciplinarity, scholarship and subjectivities, remains somewhat invisible and is therefore frequently taken for granted and assumed to be a transparent medium, leading to a fading from view in policy, research and development.

The Digital Invisible

A further feature of the learning outcomes model, and the absence of reference to prevailing mediatic conditions, leads to further elision of the digital in particular.

This seems to also reinforce the notion of the digital as a transparent and neutral tool – an idea critiqued later in this book – as opposed to viewing the digital as an active agent which is in a reciprocal relationship with not only what is learned but how it is learned in terms of engagement. Contemporary Higher Education involves a combination of the digital and the analogue as discussed above, and it is saturated with the digital, both on and off campus. However, arguably, the field has been slow to reject the 'digital dualist' conception of face-to-face learning versus e-learning, and, as a result, the digitally permeated and altered nature of campus engagement and independent study has arguably been under-researched and underestimated.

Returning to the lecture as an example, as argued in Gourlay (2012), this is seen as the prototypical face-to-face and embodied university encounter, and it is often used to denote a contrast with the supposedly disembodied realm of the digital. Partly as a result of this, in addition to the prevalence of the active learning discourse discussed above, it is often derided as retrograde. Leaving aside the various possible responses to this critique, one point is worth noting – the 'old-fashioned' lecture is in fact saturated with the digital. This includes the uses of online material and devices in preparation, and the mainstreaming of virtual learning environments, along with the increasing expectation that these should be made available in advance of the live class. The lecturer speaks to a group of co-present people, but alongside a screen, which in large lecture theatres may be much larger than the human-scale chalkboard used in the past for writing or other non-digital use. This screen is used to project pre-prepared digital multimodal texts in the form of slides or other texts, images or videos. The students are likely to be using portable networked digital devices during the lecture; these may be used for note taking, or for searching for other academic – or indeed non-academic – texts (including on social media). As a module progresses, students will be required to prepare coursework, which is achieved through predominantly digital means. Even the handwritten texts of the live exam are prepared for using digital media. This is not to say that *all* meaning-making practices are digital in the contemporary university, but rather, as we have seen earlier, digitally mediated practices are likely to be intertwined with print literacy practices in a complex assemblage. In that sense, as argued in Chapter 2, the digital is not a separate realm, but one which permeates the material in society more broadly, and also in the practices of Higher Education, even those practices derided as pre-digital and labelled retrograde as a result.

Cope and Kalantzis (2009) investigate the extent of the changes which have come about in the university as a result of digitisation. In particular, they seek to address the question of the extent to which digital technologies '. . . reproduce the knowledge systems of the half-millennium long history of the modern university', or disrupt them. In their analysis, they do not support one or other of these extreme positions, but instead point out the continuities and similarities between pre-digital and digital texts, such as the PDF, which is essentially a facsimile of a printed document. They also point out the similarity between supposedly transformational hypertext, and the centuries-old practice of cross-referencing using catalogue listing. They (somewhat provocatively) ask:

> What is the hypertextual link other than a way of making the same old distinction of individual authorship, delineating the boundaries between one piece of intellectual property and the next, and a sign of deference to the authorities on which a text is based? As for the much-vaunted novelty of the 'virtual', what more is this than a reincarnation of the modes of representation of distant people, places and objects that made books so alluring from the moment they became cheaply and widely accessible? Also, books and their distribution systems, no less than today's networked communities, allowing the creation of dispersed communities of expertise?
>
> *(Cope and Kalantzis 2009:5)*

However, they do concede that the digital has brought about considerable changes. One that they highlight is 'economies of cultural and epistemic scale' (*ibid.*), in which the number of copies of a text is no longer limited by the cost of production and distribution, leading to a proliferation in the sheer quantity and range of texts and resources available online. They also mention increased multimodality and the potential for academia to move away from the dominance of linguistic text as its primary means of representation. (This tendency is explored in detail in the literature elsewhere, e.g. Andrews and England 2012, Archer and Brewer 2016.) However, the main implication that Cope and Kalantzis emphasise is the changed relationship between the author and reader (also explored in Kalantzis and Cope 2008). They point out the multi-authored nature of sites like Wikipedia, platforms such as Google Docs, digital annotation applications that allow the reader to intervene in a digital text, the public nature of blogs as opposed to private diaries, and the potential to be a participant in video games as opposed to a viewer of television, among other examples. They see this as a rebalancing of agency between author and reader, towards 'reflexive co-construction' (Cope and Kalantzis 2009:8). In this regard, we can have insight into the various ways that the digital is subtly changing practices in education – however, it appears that these nuances are often lost, falling between the cracks of overhyped claims from the TEL community on one hand, and a rendering of the digital to a somewhat invisible status in the mainstream curriculum on the other. In all of this, the detail and complexity of student engagement with the digital can be missed.

A further area where the influence of the digital can be seen in students' practices is the relationship between informal social media use and academic digital literacies. Bhatt (2012) reports on a study into the relationship between personal and classroom digital literacy. Using the notion of the 'literacy event' (Heath 1983), Bhatt found college students' vernacular digital literacies related to social media use were 'translated' (Latour 2005) into digital literacy practices associated with academic learning, despite efforts on the part of the college to delineate and 'purify' (Bhatt 2012:297) what is, and what is not, acceptable digital media practice in the context of the college. The influence of social media on academic practice can also be seen with academic staff. Costa (2013) explored the 'habitus' of lecturers, and found a strong relationship between their 'online social capital' and their scholarship practices, citing practices such as crowdsourcing, open-access publication and blogging. Textual practices are also changing, as Fransman and Andrews (2012) discuss in their consideration of how rhetoric and representation are shifting in the digital age, highlighting multimodality and the rapid and widespread dissemination of texts enabled by digital technologies, leading to a blurring of traditional genres. Knox and Bayne (2013) explore this further in their examination of the 'profusion' of multimodal literacies observed in their MOOC, which they read as '. . . a complex series of socio-material entanglements, in which human beings and technologies each played a constituent part' (Knox and Bayne 2013:1). It is clear that the digital is bringing about new openings and possibilities for representation and subjectivities, which can be seen in the shifting and dynamic nature of contemporary scholarly practice. However, crucially, these are used selectively, and do not appear to be entirely supplanting established practices. Instead they become intertwined, and change appears to be more subtle than the predictions of transformation discussed above.

Conclusions

In this chapter, we have argued that two often-neglected elements are entangled in complex threads running throughout contemporary Higher Education practice: meaning-making and the digital. Looking at the construct of learning outcomes, we argued that the emphasis on student activity – although appearing to focus on student engagement – is expressed at a largely abstracted level, where the fundamentally semiotic nature of the enactment of learning processes and the demonstration of learning outcomes is lost from view. We also argued that, despite the hype, the pervasive and more subtle influence of the digital on student engagement – online, offline, in class and in private study – is also elided. We concluded that these lacunae are related. In both, there is an assumption that Higher Education and learning somehow sit outside of meaning-making practices and mediatic conditions, and that these should be regarded as transparent, neutral and frictionless, whose function is to act as empty receptacles for the expression of learning, which somehow takes place elsewhere. The 'grain' and mess of slowly-emerging, often faltering, complex and messy meaning-making practices is rendered smooth in these seductively tidy models of rarefied outcomes. The specificity of entanglements with the devices and artefacts of inscription and meaning-making – digital and analogue – are filed away under tools for the user to access, instead of being recognised for their intra-agential natures and deeply intertwined relationships and entanglements with students and engagement itself.

In the next chapter we will move the focus away from these sector-level accounts of student engagement, and look at how engagement is described and delineated in the mainstream discipline-based curriculum, shifting our focus back to the digital. We will begin by taking a critical look at how notions of generational differences have dominated how we have come to think of student engagement with the digital, and also at how skills and resultant frameworks have come to play a persistent role in how we think about engagement, scholarship, the digital and ultimately the university itself.

References

Andrews, R. and England, J. (Eds.). 2012. *The SAGE Handbook of Digital Dissertations and Theses*. London: SAGE.

Archer, A. and Brewer, E. (Eds.). 2016. *Multimodality in Higher Education*. Leiden, The Netherlands: Brill.

Bazerman, C., Little, J., Bethel, L., Chavkin, T., Fouquette, D. and Garufis, J. 2005. *Reference Guide to Writing Across the Curriculum*. Anderson, SC: Parlor Press.

Bhatt, I. 2012. Digital literacy practices and their layered multiplicity. *Educational Media International* 49(4), 289–301.

Biggs, J. 1996. Enhancing learning through constructive alignment. *Higher Education* 32(3), 347–364.

Biggs, J. B. 2011. *Teaching for quality learning at university: What the student does*. New York: McGraw-Hill Education.

Biggs, J. and Collis, K. 1982. *Evaluating the Quality of Learning: The SOLO Taxonomy (Structure of the Observed Learning Outcome)*. London: Academic Press.

Bloom, B. S., Engelhart, M. D., Furst, E. J., Hill, W. H. and Krathwohl, D. R. (1956). *Taxonomy of educational objectives, handbook I: The cognitive domain*. New York: David McKay Co.

Bologna Working Group. 2005. A Framework for Qualifications of the European Higher Education Area. *Bologna Working Group Report on Qualifications Frameworks (Copenhagen, Danish Ministry of Science, Technology and Innovation)*. http://ecahe.eu/w/index.php/Framework_for_Qualifications_of_the_European_Higher_Education_Area#Source [Accessed 10 Aug 2017].

Cohen. 1987. Instructional alignment: searching for a magic bullet. *Educational Researcher* 16(8), 16–20.

Cope, B. and Kalantzis, M. 2009. The role of the internet in changing knowledge ecologies. *Arbor* 185(737), 521–530.

Costa, C. 2013. The habitus of digital scholars. *Research in Learning Technology* 21(0), 21274.

Fransman, J. and Andrews, R. 2012. Rhetoric and the politics of representation and communication in the digital age. *Learning, Media and Technology* 37(2), 125–130.

Fry, H., Ketteridge, S. and Marshall, S. 2015. *A Handbook for Teaching and Learning in Higher Education: Enhancing Academic Practice* (4th Ed.). Abingdon: Routledge.

Gourlay, L. 2012. Cyborg ontologies and the lecturer's voice: a posthuman reading of the 'face-to-face'. *Learning, Media and Technology* 37(2), 198–211.

Havnes, A. and Proitz, T. 2016. Why use learning outcomes in higher education? Exploring the grounds for academic resistance and reclaiming the value of unexpected learning. *Educational Assessment, Evaluation and Accountability* 28(3), 2015–2223.

Heath, S. 1983. *Ways with Words: Language, Life and Work in Communities and Classrooms.* Cambridge: Cambridge University Press.

Ivanic, R. 1998. *Writing and Identity: The Discoursal Construction of Identity in Academic Writing.* Amsterdam: John Benjamins.

Jewitt, C. 2009. *The Routledge Handbook of Multimodal Analysis.* London: Routledge.

Kalantzis, M. and Cope, B. 2008. *New Learning: Elements of a Science of Education.* Cambridge: Cambridge University Press.

Knox, J. and Bayne, S. 2013. Multimodal profusion in the literacies of the Massive Open Online Course. *Research in Learning Technology* 21(0), 21422.

Kress, G. 2009. *Multimodality: A Social Semiotic Approach to Contemporary Communication.* New York: Routledge.

Latour, B. 2005. *Reassembling the Social: An Introduction to Actor-Network-Theory.* Oxford: Oxford University Press.

Lea, M. 1998. Academic literacies and learning in higher education: constructing knowledge through texts and experience. *Studies in the Education of Adults* 30(2), 156–171.

Lea, M. and Steirer, B. 2009. Lecturers' everyday writing as professional practice in the university as workplace: new insights into academic identities. *Studies in Higher Education* 34(4), 417–428.

Lea, M. and Street, B. 1998. Student writing in higher education: An academic literacies approach. *Studies in higher education* 23(2), 157–172.

Lillis, T. 2001. *Student Writing: Access, Regulation, Desire.* Abingdon: Routledge.

Lillis, T., Harrington, K., Lea, M. and Mitchell, S. (Eds.) 2015. *Working with Academic Literacies: Case Studies Towards Transformative Practice.* Fort Collins, CO: The WAC Clearinghouse.

Marton, K. and Saljo, R. 1976a. On qualitative differences in learning: I – outcome and process. *British Journal of Educational Psychology* 46(1), 4–11.

Marton, K. and Saljo, R. 1976b. On qualitative differences in learning II – outcome as a function of the learner's conception of the task. *British Journal of Educational Psychology* 46(2), 115–127.

QAA. 2014. *UK Quality Code for Higher Education.* www.qaa.ac.uk/en/Publications/Documents/qualifications-frameworks.pdf [Accessed 10th August 2017].

Race, P. 2014. *The Lecturer's Toolkit: A Practical Guide to Assessment, Learning and Teaching* (4th Ed.). Abingdon: Routledge.

Ramsden, P. 2003. *Learning to Teach in Higher Education* (2nd Ed.). Abingdon: Routledge-Falmer.

Wingate, U. 2006. Doing away with 'study skills'. *Teaching in Higher Education* 11(4), 457–469.

4

THE TROUBLE WITH FRAMEWORKS

The previous chapter focused on the superordinate level of sector-wide constructs concerning student engagement, critiquing these as overly abstracted and neglectful of meaning-making and digital mediation. This chapter develops this discussion by shifting the focus away from institutions and systems, back towards the digital and towards how students have been categorised in terms of their digital engagement. A series of influential positions in this area is reviewed, giving rise to questions about whether any kind of framework is fit for the job of describing student engagement or experience.

Ruptures and Binaries in Our Stories about Students

Throughout the first decade of the 21st century, discussions of students were shaped by a series of influential generational discourses. In educational contexts, these included discussions of the 'Net Generation' (Tapscott 1998), 'millennials' (Howe and Strauss 2000) and 'digital natives' (Prensky 2001a). A common feature across all of these discussions was the way that they created sharp 'us and them' divides, which emphasised the alleged differences between youth – who were homogeneously characterised as having been 'born digital' – and the adults who might have to teach them. Authors such as Tapscott and Prensky advanced the argument that the way in which this generation had grown up with technology had fundamentally reshaped the way they interacted with each other. The consequence of this, they proposed, was that established forms of education were just no longer relevant to them, even on a biological level.

It is very likely that our students' brains have physically changed – and are different from ours – as a result of how they grew up. Educators [. . .] can choose to ignore their eyes, ears and intuition, pretend the Digital Native/ Digital Immigrant issue does not exist, and continue to use their suddenly-much-less-effective traditional methods until they retire and the Digital Natives take over. Or they can choose instead to accept the fact that they have become Immigrants into a new Digital world.

(Prensky 2001b)

This apocalyptic framing of a generational rupture – a 'singularity', Prensky suggested – captured the imagination of many educators and policymakers, spurring yet another round of investment in new technologies for education, which at that point meant social media sites, wikis and virtual worlds (Selwyn 2009). In other words, the rhetorical effect of this construction of a social division was to make those in education who held the budget believe themselves doomed to obsolescence, unless they used their limited resources to fuel the profits of technology developers.

Links between social anxiety about youth and the market are nothing new, however. Buckingham (2013) has argued that there is at least a century's worth of precedent for this kind of fear that youth cultures have become impossible for adults to understand. He draws attention to the way in which the very idea of 'a generation' is both an historical and a cultural construct, something used to characterise cohorts born within a time frame (or around some traumatic event), but also something that potential members of this generation can invoke, in order to position themselves as having some kind of shared identity. Critically, however, it also becomes something that marketers can use to segment society in order to create and manage demand for particular products. The neatness of the us/them binary orders the chaos of society in a way that enables advertising and sales, with distinctive and targeted rhetorical strategies.

However, the neatness of this binary is a fiction. When researchers attempted to explore these apocalyptic claims, evidence to support them proved elusive. Bennett, Maton and Kervin (2008), for example, set out to explore this generational divide sociologically, and found evidence of broad trends towards increasing levels of technology use, but no sharp generational differences. Indeed, they concluded, there were important variations in patterns of technology use *within* each of the supposed generations, undermining any claims about the homogeneity of the groups. As a result, they concluded that 'rather than being empirically and theoretically informed, the debate can be likened to an academic form of a "moral panic"'(*ibid.* 775).

The supposed homogeneity becomes even harder to credit once studies from across the Global South start to be taken into account – something not adequately considered by the North American authors who constructed these generational divides. Studies in South Africa, for example, showed that the assumed characteristics of 'digital natives' more accurately accounted only for relatively affluent individuals – a 'digital elite' – and the normative assumptions underlying these discourses were subsequently characterised as a kind of 'digital apartheid' that could actually serve to deepen existing divides within societies (Brown and Czerniewicz

2010). Faced with these kinds of challenges, even Prensky eventually withdrew from the sharp binaries that he had developed – not admitting their error, but conceding that they had grown 'less relevant'. Instead, he proposed focusing on 'digital wisdom', a rather superficial trans-human reading of digitally mediated social practices (2009). However, this never received the same level of traction that his earlier, more simplistic framework achieved.

The rhetorical appeal of reducing society's complexity to easily managed binaries may be strong, but as this example serves to illustrate, things remain stubbornly complicated. This pattern has repeated many times in the field of educational technology, and can be seen throughout discussions of the digital within universities, in particular in terms of the construct 'digital literacies'.

Frameworks for Digital Literacies

When the term 'digital literacy' was coined, Gilster defined it as:

> The ability to understand and use information in multiple formats from a wide range of sources when it is presented via computers.
>
> *(Gilster 1997:1)*

This initial framing is remarkably inclusive, even vague – a problem it shares with many definitions and frameworks in educational technology (Oliver 2016). These frequently rely on accretion and aggregation, rather than exclusion, in order to build a definition, commonly building up lists of things that count as part of a category or concept, or adding new examples that can illustrate it.

It is interesting that this short form of Gilster's definition presents digital literacy as a singular thing – 'the ability' – which suggests an either/or binary, one that is more inclusive than the generational discourses around digital natives, but that is equally divisive. However, to take this at face value would be to oversimplify his analysis, which concerns the development of reading and writing practices around hypertexts, including the emergence of what would now be referred to as multimodality (Kress 2009). His focus was relatively specific, leading him to specify digital literacy in terms of what he described as four competencies: knowledge assembly, evaluating information content, searching the internet, and navigating hypertext (Gilster 1997).

Since Gilster's original definition, there have been repeated attempts to make the idea more precise – and many of these have involved the creation of taxonomies or lists of features. These have both shaped and been shaped by recent educational policies. For example, some have echoed the trend of shifting the focus towards the learner, so that the definition focuses less on technology. Bawden, for example, emphasised:

> the ideas and mindsets, within which particular skills and competences operate, and [. . .] information and information resources, in whatever format.
>
> *(Bawden 2008:19)*

However, many others have remained technologically oriented, resulting in superficial lists with little long-term value.

> These formulations still tend to focus on technical 'know-how' that is relatively easy to acquire and on skills that are likely to become obsolete fairly rapidly.
>
> *(Buckingham 2010:60–61)*

Both of these developments pose problems. Whether the definition is based on features of technology that must be mastered, or attributes of learners, this desire to simplify and organise digital literacies risks losing sight of important aspects of students' engagements with technology.

Lankshear and Knobel (2006) have argued that developments of the idea of digital literacy have relied upon 'standardised operations', codifying actions down to the level of keystrokes in an attempt to reduce ambiguity and make digital literacy easy to test. At worst, this can result in simplistic binaries – literate/not literate – or at best some measurable continuum. Irrespective of the precise form, however, they argue that such definitions typically rely on modernist, positivistic assumptions, specifying digital literacy in terms of *information*, which is then assessed in terms of *truth*, and is understood to be generic, rather than shaped in powerful ways by social practice, social context and discourses.

> We should think of 'digital literacy' not as something unitary, and certainly not as some finite 'competency' or 'skill' – or even as a set of competencies or skills. Rather, it means we should think of 'digital literacy' as shorthand for the myriad social practices and conceptions of engaging in meaning making mediated by texts that are produced, received, distributed, exchanged etc., via digital codification. Digital literacy is really *digital literacies*.
>
> *(Lankshear and Knobel 2006:17)*

These kinds of issues persist, however, as can be shown by following the development of the definitions of digital literacy that shaped the research project described in this book. These issues trace back to a definition developed by the European Union funded DigEuLit project. The approach taken within this project once again relied on listing examples of things that, together, might constitute digital literacy:

> Digital Literacy is the awareness, attitude and ability of individuals to appropriately use digital tools and facilities to identify, access, manage, integrate, evaluate, analyse and synthesise digital resources, construct new knowledge, create media expressions, and communicate with others, in the context of specific life situations, in order to enable constructive social action; and to reflect upon this process.
>
> *(Martin and Grudziecki 2006:255)*

This appears to cover all areas of contemporary digitally mediated life; it is not restricted to academic forms of literacy. This made it an obvious point of reference for the projects in the JISC programme that will be described in Chapter 5, which was motivated by the wider policy agenda of producing graduates fit to work in industry. Indeed, their definition was directly influenced by European policy (European Commission 2003), which identified it as 'a prerequisite for creativity, innovation and entrepreneurship', as well as enabling citizens to 'participate fully in society'.

Martin and Grudziecki developed their definition using a three-level framework, differentiating digital competence, digital usage and digital transformation. They define competence in terms of functional skills, knowledge, aptitudes and attitudes, applicable in many situations and usable to achieve a range of different goals. However, they moved immediately from this inclusive but general formulation, to consider 13 processes of digital literacy, effectively creating a list of verbs that could be applied to 'digital resources'. These include accessing, evaluating, organising, analysing, synthesising, communicating and reflecting. The digital resources themselves were 'considered in the most inclusive way', and illustrated by providing a list of examples.

This marks a clear step forward from the kinds of binary classifications noted earlier. The 13 different processes would allow, for example, a considerable range of individual profiles to be described, even if each individual classification was in itself a binary of achieved/not achieved. However, although competencies might appear fixed and certain as a result of the way they are tested and then talked about, in practice they are better understood as being fluid and contingent, and dependent on the dynamics of specific situations (Mulcahy 2000). This suggests that no matter how extensive a competency framework was, it would not be able to indicate prospectively with any certainty what a given individual might be capable of. In this regard, these frameworks share the shortcomings highlighted in the previous chapter in relation to learning outcomes.

It is also interesting to note that this formulation marks a subtle shift away from Gilster's focus on 'information', although their emphasis remains on the creation of knowledge and on communication, with an acknowledgement of the connection between this and 'social action'. Notably, this level of their framework remains abstract, with these actions 'free-floating', devoid of any specific context. This suggests, unhelpfully, that if an individual *has* a particular competence, then this persists in some timeless, decontextualised way.

Their second level – digital usage – is where context re-emerges, understood in terms of professional or 'domain' or 'other' life-contexts. Referencing communities of practice, they propose that:

> Users draw upon relevant digital competences and elements specific to the profession, domain or other life-context. Each user brings to this exercise

his/her own history and personal/professional development. Digital usages are thus shaped by the requirements of the situation.

(Martin and Grudziecki 2006:257)

Here, some consideration is given to the social contexts of practices, but materiality remains conspicuously absent, and there is no discussion of how the verbs operating at the level of competence may be modulated or enacted. The third and final level is only outlined briefly, indexing instances where 'the digital usages which have been developed enable innovation and creativity, and stimulate significant change within the professional or knowledge domain', once more celebrating the 'transformative', as discussed in Chapter 2.

This framework – oriented towards free-floating individuals who are able to apply generic competencies across a range of situations, and whose actions may be contextualised socially but not materially – featured in the background report that scoped work on the JISC programme (Beetham, McGill and Littlejohn 2009), and through that, it influenced the formulation of the initial model of digital literacies that the individual projects then worked with (Beetham 2010). Here, the following definition was offered:

> Digital literacy defines those capabilities which fit an individual for living, learning and working in a digital society.

This is a broad definition – one suitably inclusive for inviting projects into a national programme, but perhaps less well suited to an analysis of the day-to-day lives of students. The definition was accompanied by a model (see Figure 4.1), consisting of a pyramid built of four layers: access, skills, social practices and identity. The use of a pyramid is intended to imply 'a developmental sequence' (Sharpe and Beetham 2010:88), which they propose is analogous to Maslow's hierarchy of learning needs – although in this particular alternative account, the highest level (identity) is replaced with 'creative appropriation'.

Sharpe and Beetham (2010) go on to explain the logic of this. They propose that 'without reliable, convenient and cost-effective access, none of the other attributes of effective e-learners can be brought into play' (*ibid.* 90). Here, the situatedness of social action is acknowledged, but in terms of barriers and constraints – an account of 'permissions', which indexes wider discussions of soft determinism within the field of educational technology (Oliver 2011). The subsequent layer consists of 'generic' technical, information and learning skills – functional actions, which are described in terms of being 'mastered', echoing the kinds of contextless competencies Martin and Grudziecki (2006) discussed. This suggests a binary of skills either being held or not held; or more charitably, perhaps, that there might be some continuum of proficiency with which a skill is possessed. Although this marks a modest development of the kinds of complexity discussed for the above

Defining digital literacy: a general model

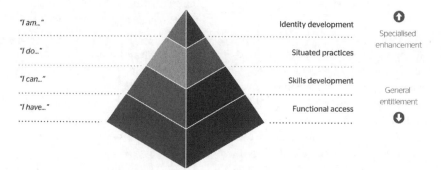

FIGURE 4.1   The pyramid model of digital literacies (from JISC 2014)

competencies, it nevertheless remains simply linear and progressive, devoid of context and immune to the influence of time.

The third layer, practices, is described in terms of informed choices from a repertoire of possible approaches made in response to situational needs. This reintroduces socially specific contexts, but still leaves agency firmly located with the 'tool-using' learner.

The final stage, as noted earlier, varies depending on the source of the model. In the documents that framed the JISC projects, this was identity – a complex and fluid concept, which was not elaborated within the project documentation. However, the LLiDA (Learning Literacies for the Digital Age) report (Beetham, McGill and Littlejohn 2009:3) that provided a foundation for the programme, did develop the idea of identity, explaining this in terms of 'recognising technology practice as diverse and constitutive of personal identity, including identity in different peer, subject and workplace communities, and individual styles of participation', suggesting links to work in the tradition of New Literacy Studies. A later version of the model – published by JISC after the programme was complete – modifies this label, linking identity to 'specialised enhancement' (JISC 2014). This appears to imply that identity is an advanced and specialised state, as opposed to a construct which can refer to individuals more broadly – an idea that fits with the notion of a progressive, linear development, but which is contradicted by literature from New Literacy Studies, such as that exploring the identities of students who feel marginalised by mainstream academic practices (e.g. Lillis 2001). As this work illustrates, the development of identity need not involve refinement and inclusion, but can equally consist of exclusion.

In the other version of the model, the alternative highest level – 'creative appropriation' – is outlined but not fully developed, echoing the brevity with which Martin and Grudziecki (2006) discussed transformative levels of digital literacy. The emphasis within this model is on learners' use of technologies to take control of their own learning, acting in ways that were not anticipated by the course or tutor. The link between this model and New Literacy Studies is interesting, given the critical perspective that tradition has taken towards the idea of skills. The foundational definition of 'academic literacies' (Lea and Street 1998) rests on the explicit rejection of the skills model of student academic writing, which was prevalent at the time. This was motivated by the lack of attention that the skills approach paid to social, disciplinary and individual practices and identities.

From a New Literacies perspective, social practices cannot and should not be separated from the other layers in the pyramid, because they subsume the others. For example, 'access' only makes sense in specific situations: access to some thing, for some purpose, within specific social situations. Further, the situated perspective adopted within New Literacy Studies means that all social practices would be understood as creative appropriations, even if some might be more conventional than others.

Positioning 'identity' as the highest layer is similarly problematic. These elements are constructed as sequential and hierarchical, each resting on another in what appears to be a causal configuration, as if each new layer is in some way the product or consequence of the preceding ones. However, reliable, cost-effective and convenient access could easily be understood as a consequence of a learner's privilege (Holley and Oliver 2009). As a result, it could easily be argued that identity is prior to access – since socioeconomic status, gender and a range of other aspects of subjectivity are known to facilitate, limit or deny access to digital devices, both in the UK and worldwide.

It could also be argued, even more convincingly, that situated practice is prior to all engagement. As founding ethnographic studies of situated literacies showed us (e.g. Street 1998), literacies emerge and are generated *by* situated practice, rather than being practised in isolation and then applied. Instead, this model appears to see situated practice and expression of identity as 'capstone' achievements, which are reached as an endpoint through apparently asocial and unsituated processes of functional access and skills development.

As an illustration of this, after working with this model, Bennett (2014) concluded that because an academic's evolving identity as a teacher might require them to engage with social practices that they were previously unfamiliar with, very few would move from seeking access towards the development of a 'digital practitioner' identity in a linear or even a consistent way. All of this is consistent with critiques of Maslow's presumed hierarchy. For example, Tay and Diener (2011) showed that the hierarchy is not consistent internationally, and noted that even Maslow saw his proposed ordering as 'soft' rather than determining behaviour.

As we will outline in Chapter 5, the study discussed in this book was funded by JISC as part of a programme of institutional projects. On the basis of these projects, and other accompanying work, JISC developed an advisory document for institutions, 'Quick Guide: Developing Students' Digital Literacy' (JISC 2014). Here, we will review this document in order to explore the extent to which the issues identified above were addressed, and to consider further alternatives.

The strapline of the JISC quick guide document is: 'Digital literacies – the capabilities which fit someone for living, learning and working in a digital society', drawing directly on Beetham's 2010 definition, which was used as the basis for the programme. It is noteworthy, however, that in the body of the report, JISC uses both the singular and the plural of literacy as the guiding concept, glossing literacies as 'capacities'. The opening paragraph goes on to state:

> Digital literacy is a broad and holistic concept that embraces much more than the functional IT skills that students need to survive in a digital society. Although many students are skilled technology users, they do not usually come into further or higher education armed with all the digital competencies they need to thrive in their academic lives and in employment. This highlights a key role for universities and colleges to support students to develop differentiated, specialised and advanced digital literacy skills, above the general core entitlement that students expect. We develop literacy skills over time, becoming increasingly proficient and fluent with support and practice. Beetham and Sharpe's framework (2010) highlights how this developmental process relates to digital literacy – from access and functional skills to higher level capabilities. Crucially, it recognises that digital literacies will vary according to context so it also reflects how individuals can be motivated to develop new skills and practices in different situations.
>
> *(JISC 2014:1)*

Terminology – in this area of educational thought as in others – is an important marker of underlying theoretical stance. What is interesting about this paragraph is that it begins by rejecting the notion of 'functional skills' as a sufficient definition and focus, and instead argues for a 'holistic' concept of digital literacy. As such, it appears to have incorporated some of the critical concerns raised above, of the need to address not just free-floating learners but also the wider network of people and artefacts with which they are studying. However, the document then points out that students may not have the competencies they need – contradicting the wider, more situated use of the term 'literacies', which as discussed above, explicitly rejects the competencies model of engagement. The document goes on to propose that universities need to develop 'digital literacy skills' beyond the core student entitlement. This is striking, as it creates a portmanteau term which combines two entirely contradictory conceptual understandings of engagement and practice – the literacies perspective, and the skills perspective.

Of course, it must be borne in mind that this document is intended for policymakers and practitioners, and as such it may have been deemed helpful rhetorically to use the term 'skills', since this is widely recognised across the sector and might help to bring the work of the projects within the programme to a wider audience, where 'literacy' might have been deemed unfamiliar. However, we would argue that this also gives rise to a lack of coherence around the whole framework, which appears as a result to fall somewhere between the two positions.

The following statements within the document then refer to 'literacy skills' as developing over time with practice. Although there is a recognition that student needs are likely to change, this element of the statement seems strongly rooted in a skills perspective which sees engagement as essentially cumulative, fragmented, linear and mastery based. As discussed later in this book, these assumptions were not substantiated by the data in the project, which often saw students dip into technologies with little or no practice, and also saw them drop or forget how to use certain platforms as they became irrelevant to their needs. The day-to-day nature of contemporary student engagement, on the basis of this data, seems closer in nature to a constantly shifting, messy and improvised *bricolage*, than a set of steadily improving discrete and structured skills. It also, as discussed in Chapter 3 in relation to skills frameworks more generally, still regards the human as the sole agent of digital engagement.

The document goes on to present a diagrammatic model, showing 'the seven elements of digital literacies', as shown in Figure 4.2 (on page 48).

This model is presented as a matrix as opposed to a cumulative set of steps, and consists of a range of elements which are seen as components of digital literacies. It helpfully includes reading and writing, although 'media literacy' is the heading here as opposed to academic literacy. Learning is still framed in terms of skills in the diagram. However, overall, this model seems more congruent with a literacies perspective than the pyramid model that precedes it – the elements are described in terms of verbs which refer to practices, which is itself a significant change. The document goes on to make a series of very helpful points about the importance of context, and the need to engage staff and students in dialogue around these practices – it clearly includes some helpful elements, and represents a positive move forward from the more linear model presented prior to the programme.

However, the relationship between the two models is not elaborated, nor is the basis for either justified within the guide in terms of theory or research. Instead they are implicitly presented to the reader as fact. As a consequence, the overall impression is that the position taken in the guide is not explicitly theorised or research informed. This lack of theoretical coherence or research base, combined with the apparently closed and generic nature of the models and categories, risks a relapse to common-sense accounts, leading us back to a skills model by the back door. It is unclear whether the second diagram is a descriptive, theoretical model of what digital literacies consists of, or an aspirational tick list of what an idealised user *should* master – this is one of the issues identified in Chapter 3, accompanying the switch in status from descriptions of specific learners' experiences to a normative account of what other learners ought to do. In addition, the sites of practice and

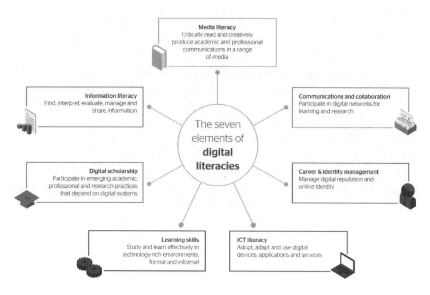

FIGURE 4.2 JISC's seven elements of digital literacies

development are elided, and again the human user is placed in a central, but simultaneously unsituated, position. Overall, although the post-programme document and models demonstrate progress towards recognising the centrality of practices, changing needs and contexts, they stop short of achieving a clean break from a skills model or pursuing a more radical reconceptualisation of what student engagement with the digital might mean. We will attempt to propose such an alternative model later in the book.

A further parallel model seeking to account for students' digital engagement has been developed in the context of information literacy. Information literacy has tended to be treated somewhat separately from academic and digital literacies, although, as the JISC model suggests, this has changed in recent years. The Society of College, University and National Libraries (SCONUL) represents libraries in Ireland and the UK, and it has developed a model of information literacies known as the 'Seven Pillars of Information Literacy'. As with the JISC model discussed above, this has been elaborated in an open-access document (SCONUL Working Group on Information Literacy 2011), which begins with some background to the model:

> In 1999, The SCONUL Working Group on Information Literacy published 'Information skills in higher education: a SCONUL position paper' (SCONUL 1999), introducing the Seven Pillars of Information Skills model. Since then, the model has been adopted by librarians and teachers around the world as a means of helping them to deliver information skills to their learners. However, in 2011 we live in a very different information

world and while the basic principles underpinning the original Seven Pillars model remain valid, it was felt that the model needed to be updated and expanded to reflect more clearly the range of different terminologies and concepts which we now understand as 'Information Literacy'.

(SCONUL Working Group on Information Literacy 2011:1)

It is noteworthy that this model, like the JISC one, has moved away from the construct 'information skills' towards a 'literacies' framing. It goes on to define 'information literacy' as follows:

Information Literacy is an umbrella term which encompasses concepts such as digital, visual and media literacies, academic literacy, information handling, information skills, data curation and data management . . . Information literate people will demonstrate an awareness of how they gather, use, manage, synthesise and create information and data in an ethical manner and will have the information skills to do so effectively.

(SCONUL Working Group on Information Literacy 2011:2)

It is interesting to note that SCONUL regards information literacies as the superordinate term, with digital and academic literacies positioned as constituent elements; for JISC, information and other literacies were subordinate to digital literacies. This definition focuses on literacies, which are exemplified with reference to practices. However, once again, the term 'skills' is used to conceptualise what is required in order to enact literacies as practices. There is then inconsistency between the holistic model of the person and their practices, and the fragmented, linear, mastery model of the individual skills that are assumed to constitute this – although there is at least some recognition of the world changing around learners.

Developing as an information literate person is a continuing, holistic process with often simultaneous activities or processes which can be encompassed within the Seven Pillars of Information Literacy. Within each 'pillar' an individual can develop from 'novice' to 'expert' as they progress through their learning life, although, as the information world itself is constantly changing and developing, it is possible to move down a pillar as well as progress up it.

(SCONUL Working Group on Information Literacy 2011:2)

SCONUL goes further to introduce the idea of 'an information literate person'. This suggests a recognisable category, with (implicitly) defining characteristics and therefore exclusions; at this point, the potentially destabilising experience of changes to the wider 'information world' (or later, 'information landscape') is not considered. This specification of practice in terms of skills and competencies is familiar – although there is one unusual feature in the way that the framework categorises 'behaviours' as part of 'understanding'. In order to elaborate the model, each pillar is associated with a verb, which appears to relate to various categories of practice which students might engage in when working with texts and producing academic work. What is immediately apparent is the fairly high-level generic nature of the verbs, as with learning outcomes that were discussed in Chapter 3. It is also interesting to note the ordering of the pillars as a circle (see Figure 4.3), with 'identify' placed at the top. Given that circularly ordered items are conventionally read left to right, or clockwise, the effect of this ordering is to create the impression of a sequence which describes an idealised set of steps that might lead a learner through the process of producing an assignment: identify the topic, scope out the area, plan the work, gather resources, evaluate resources, manage resources, then present the work.

Although this appears uncontroversial, closer inspection reveals a series of assumptions and omissions. It either assumes that the practices involved in this process do follow this orderly, discrete and predictable set of steps, or it proposes that they should – like the JISC model, the absence of an explicit research base means it is not clear on what grounds it has been developed, and whether this is a descriptive or normative model of practice. It is also not clear at what point the student does any close reading, thinking or academic writing – the model moves directly from 'manage' to 'present', bypassing any of the necessary and central steps in between. Although a set of 'generic skills and understandings' is supplied for each pillar, these core elements of academic practice do not seem to be covered.

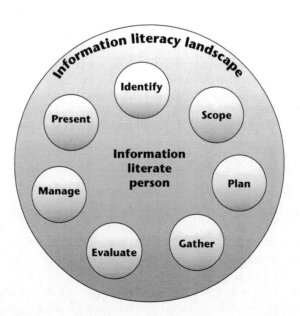

FIGURE 4.3   SCONUL Seven Pillars

Instead, academic work seems to be reduced to information retrieval, processing and presentation.

SCONUL has subsequently published a review of how the model has been received (Goldstein 2015), which acknowledges criticisms of the original model that was developed in 1999. Particularly relevant here is the recognition that the focus of the initial model was too heavy on skills, and overly based on the views of library practitioners, with a subsequent neglect of social context and the tendency towards developing models that privilege what can be measured (e.g. Andretta 2006, Andretta, Pope and Walton 2008). Goldstein quotes Boon *et al.* who suggest that information literacy frameworks:

> . . . identify a potential curriculum for teaching information literacy, and one might expect them to draw on relevant research in pedagogy, information behaviour and social informatics to define content and influence course design. This is often not the case, however, as these frameworks [. . .] have been produced by library and information science practitioners, rather than academics and/or researchers and were not devised through the use of an applied research methodology [. . .] Deriving from the experience of LIS practitioners, the information literacy frameworks reflect the conceptions of those practitioners, but do little to illuminate the conceptions and experiences of other groups involved in information literacy education.
>
> *(Boon, Johnson and Webber 2007 in Goldstein 2015:4)*

In contrast, Goldstein's review indicates that the responses in the sector were favourable towards the 2011 version discussed above. He reports that it has been praised for its flexibility, particular since the addition of five specialist lenses and student-facing guides. No criticisms of the current model are made in the review, which Goldstein describes as 'light-touch', although he recommends that the lenses should be developed and refined.

The SCONUL framework is clearly an evolving entity, responsive to the changing and varied needs of a range of students. However, it exhibits several of the same features as the JISC model, incorporating the terminology and to some extent the insights of a literacies perspective, but yet persistently referring to literacies as abstract concepts which can only be enacted or brought into being via 'skills'. Again, this suggests a slipping back into a skills framework. A further concern is the way in which 'understanding' has been separated from 'skills', which suggests that it arises separately from practice, meaning-making and mediation. In this regard, the framework feels conceptually underdeveloped and internally contradictory. Despite laudable attempts to render the model relevant, we argue that it falls into the trap of providing another example of a fragmented skills and competencies framework, which does not reflect the interconnected nature of situated practice and student digital engagement as it emerges. This, combined with a cumulative progress-towards-mastery model of learning, oversimplifies how students actually engage with texts and meaning-making in the digital university. Further, as with the JISC model above, the framework proposes the learner as the sole human agential point, a single individual who, despite some concessions to context in that 'skills' might be rendered out of date, is portrayed once again as the 'controller' of all practice. In this regard, as with the previous model, it is built on a profoundly humanist set of assumptions about how practices unfold, and how student engagement emerges. Practice is always described at an abstract level in terms of individual skills. Other students, technologies, devices, institutions, spatiality and temporality are all rendered invisible in the model, giving the impression of a frictionless process, whose success lies solely in the hands of the student, implicitly seen as a free-floating and endlessly agentive subject.

Notions of 'learner-centredness' are visible across these models, echoing the performative notions of active learning associated with student engagement in Chapter 1. Although this is doubtless intended to be an empowering move, we argue that it serves to accentuate the underlying links between the 'information literate person' and the idealised neoliberal subject. Academic thought and work – in particular criticality – are elided in both models, which instead seem to regard academic engagement as reducible to discrete and observable processes through the deployment of skills.

Both the JISC and SCONUL models were developed by professional communities with vested interests in particular accounts of student engagement. Although both were derived from research literature at the point of their initial development, the research base is now hard to discern, and both models exhibit conceptual confusion. Given these problems, it is worth considering instead a perspective that these models have invoked, but pulled back from. Drawing on New Literacy Studies, Gillen and Barton (2010) developed a definition for a parallel research programme. This definition drew on the four components of pedagogy proposed by the New London Group: situated practice, to emphasise that learning is always connected to specific domains of activity; overt instruction, re-emphasising the value of teaching to counter contemporary fixations on learning, and, in doing so, drawing attention back to the networks of agency that constitute literacy practices; critical framing, which draws attention to the importance of power relationships in communication; and transformed practice, which sets the expectations that learners will go on to make informed and effective contributions to their social worlds. From this, they went on to propose the following definition of digital literacies:

> The constantly changing practices through which people make traceable meanings using digital technologies.
>
> *(Gillen and Barton 2010:9)*

This approach contrasts in several ways with the frameworks discussed earlier in this chapter. It is not hierarchical, and no normative assumptions are made about progress or improvement. It is historical, explicitly drawing attention to the way that practices evolve. Its scope is firmly on meaning-making, rather than the wider ambitions of previous definitions to cover 'living'. Implicit within the definition, but vital to it given its derivation from New Literacy Studies, is the understanding that 'practices' are also socially situated. Nevertheless, it has several consequences, framing the work that draws on this definition in terms of 'careful and sensitive attention to what people do with texts, how they make sense of them and use them to further their own purposes in their own learning lives' (*ibid.* 9). This focus on the day-to-day, and on the complex details of learners' lives, is what shaped the study discussed in this book, as described in the next chapter.

The Limits of Frameworks

Latour's discussion of the structural appeal of elusive 'underlying frameworks' (Latour 2005:141–156), hidden to participants in empirical work and revealed by the deductive abilities of researchers, provides a playful but important critique of the risks of moving from thoughtful empirical work to normativity. If the specificity of the framework's origins is lost, all that remains is a free-floating model, assumed to have universal applicability.

The earlier digital literacy frameworks referred to here have proved influential, although the overall direction of travel has been to move away from simplistic, categorical classifications (such as has/has not binaries), towards increasing complexity and situatedness. Simplicity is appealing, but oversimplifying limits the value of the framework, particularly in terms of its ability to support analysis or interpretation.

The pyramid model of digital literacy that framed the JISC project was originally developed from learners' accounts of what they felt enabled, or acted as barriers to, their own development (Sharpe *et al.* 2009:16). As a codification of the reported experiences of that particular group of students, the pyramid model had value. It has been widely cited since its development, suggesting that it is also of use to researchers working in this area. However, it would be a mistake to lose sight of its origins and treat it as a model that defines all students' digital literacy. It is also important to appreciate that the structure it suggests was derived empirically, rather than theoretically; the inconsistencies that can be seen within it may accurately reflect the inconsistencies in learners' accounts as they focus on different parts of their experience.

Conclusions

Decontextualised models create the impression of general relevance, but practitioners who then try to work with them face the challenge of creating meaningful links between the abstraction of the representation and what it is trying to present (de Freitas *et al.* 2008). Such models reify practice but do not define it. The process of developing a model or framework provides an important opportunity for reflection on the part of the developer – but it provides no guarantee that anyone who subsequently encounters the model will be able to understand what the author intended, or to relate it to their own practice.

For this reason, the 'careful and sensitive attention' demanded by Gillen and Barton (2010) serves as a useful counterpoint to frameworks or formal models. What this attention to practice demands is a situated process, a new act of meaning-making, which has all the reflective value of framework or model development, but without the normative baggage that completed and apparently general models can carry with them. In a manner analogous to the way that qualitative researchers have had to develop alternatives to 'validity' and 'rigour' in their work (see e.g. Tracy 2010), it may be that ideas such as richness, sincerity, credibility and resonance are better at explaining the value of frameworks and models than more positivist, normative concepts would be. As a consequence, the work discussed here will focus on detailed accounts and explicit theorisation, rather than abstraction; and the relevance of this to others will depend on the resonance of these accounts as particular individuals encounter and interpret them, rather than resting on some criterion of universality. Ultimately, it is the act of creating accounts such as these that holds the most value, so that while the narratives and interpretations presented here might inform or inspire, they should not be assumed to be an adequate substitute for careful and sensitive attention towards the reader's own situation. Calling for a situated process may address the limitations of decontextualised frameworks – but this gives rise to the question, how can we speak about students' engagement without making use of these structuring devices? This is the problem that will be considered in Chapter 11. We will work towards this question by arguing for a 'resituating' of student digital engagement with reference to our research study, through Chapters 6–9. The next chapter describes our study, the methodology and the approach taken to analysis.

References

Andretta, S. 2006. Information literacy: the new 'pedagogy of the question'. In G. Walton and A. Pope (Eds.), *Information Literacy: Recognising the Need*. Oxford: Chandos.

Andretta, S., Pope, A. and Walton, G. 2008. Information literacy education in the UK: reflections on perspectives and practical approaches of curricular integration. *Communications in Information Literacy* 2(1), 36–51. www.comminfolit.org/index.php?journal=cil&page=article&op=view&path%5b%5d=Spring2008AR3 [Accessed 10 Aug 2017].

Bawden, D. 2008. Origins and concepts of digital literacy. In C. Lankshear and M. Knobel (Eds.), *Digital Literacies: Concepts, Policies and Practices* 30. New York: Peter Lang, 17–32.

Beetham, H. 2010. *Review and Scoping Study for a Cross-JISC Learning and Digital Literacies Programme*. Bristol: JISC.

Beetham, H., McGill, L. and Littlejohn, A. 2009. *Thriving in the 21st Century: Learning Literacies for the Digital Age (LLiDA Project)*. Glasgow: The Caledonian Academy, Glasgow Caledonian University. www.caledonianacademy.net/spaces/LLiDA/uploads/Main/LLiDAreportJune09.pdf [Accessed 10 Aug 2017].

Bennett, L. 2014. Learning from the early adopters: developing the digital practitioner. *Research in Learning Technology* 22(1), 21453.

Bennett, S., Maton, K. and Kervin, L. 2008. The 'digital natives' debate: A critical review of the evidence. *British Journal of Educational Technology* 39(5), 775–786.

Boon, S., Johnson, B. and Webber, S. 2007. A phenomenographic study of English faculty's conceptions of information literacy. *Journal of Documentation* 63(2), 204–228.

Brown, C. and Czerniewicz, L. 2010. Debunking the 'digital native': beyond digital apartheid, towards digital democracy. *Journal of Computer Assisted Learning* 26(5), 357–369.

Buckingham, D. 2010. Defining digital literacy: what young people need to know about digital media. In B. Bachmair (Ed.), *Medienbildung in neuen kulturraumen.* Wiesbaden: VS Verlag fur Sozialwissenschaften, 59–72.

Buckingham, D. 2013. Is there a digital generation? In D. Buckingham and R. Willett (Eds.), *Digital Generations: Children, Young People, and the New Media.* London: Routledge, 1–13.

de Freitas, S., Oliver, M., Mee, A. and Mayes, T. 2008. The practitioner perspective on the modeling of pedagogy and practice. *Journal of Computer Assisted Learning* 24(1), 26–38.

European Commission. 2003. *eLearning: Better eLearning for Europe.* Brussels: Directorate-General for Education and Culture.

Gillen, J. and Barton, D. 2010. *Digital Literacies: A Research Briefing by the Technology Enhanced Learning Phase of the Teaching and Learning Research Programme.* London: Institute of Education. http://eprints.lancs.ac.uk/33471/1/DigitalLiteracies.pdf [Accessed 11 Jul 2017].

Gilster, P. 1997. *Digital Literacy.* New York: Wiley.

Goldstein, S. 2015. *Perceptions of the SCONUL Seven Pillars of Information Literacy: A Brief Review.* SCONUL. www.sconul.ac.uk/sites/default/files/documents/Seven%20Pillars%20Review%202015.pdf [Accessed 11 Jul 2017].

Holley, D. and Oliver, M. 2009. A private revolution: how technology is enabling students to take their work home. *Enhancing Learning in the Social Sciences* 1(3), 1–31.

Howe, N. and Strauss, W. 2000. *Millennials Rising: The Next Great Generation.* New York: Vintage.

JISC. 2014. *Quick Guide: Developing Students' Digital Literacy.* Bristol: JISC. https://digitalcapability.jiscinvolve.org/wp/files/2014/09/JISC_REPORT_Digital_Literacies_280714_PRINT.pdf [Accessed 10 Aug 2017].

Kress, G. 2009. *Multimodality: A Social Semiotic Approach to Contemporary Communication.* New York: Routledge.

Lankshear, C. and Knobel, M. 2006. Digital literacy and digital literacies: Policy, pedagogy and research considerations for education. *Nordic Journal of Digital Literacy* 1(1), 12–24. http://everydayliteracies.net/files/digital_kompetence_2006.pdf [Accessed 10 Aug 2017].

Latour, B. 2005. *Reassembling the Social: An Introduction to Actor-Network-Theory.* Oxford: Oxford University Press.

Lea, M. and Street, B. 1998. Student writing in higher education: an academic literacies approach. *Studies in Higher Education* 23(2), 157–172.

Lillis, T. 2001. *Student Writing: Access, Regulation, Desire.* Abingdon: Routledge.

Martin, A. and Grudziecki, J. 2006. DigEuLit: concepts and tools for digital literacy development. *Innovation in Teaching and Learning in Information and Computer Sciences* 5(4), 1–19.

Mulcahy, D. 2000. Turning the contradictions of competence: competency-based training and beyond. *Journal of Vocational Education and Training* 52(2), 259–280.

Oliver, M. 2011. Technological determinism in educational technology research: some alternative ways of thinking about the relationship between learning and technology. *Journal of Computer Assisted Learning* 27(5), 373–384.

Oliver, M. 2016. What is technology? In N. Rushby and D. Surry (Eds.), *The Wiley Handbook of Learning Technology*. New Jersey: Wiley-Blackwell, 35–57.

Prensky, M. 2001a. Digital natives, digital immigrants. *On the Horizon* 9(5), 1–6.

Prensky, M. 2001b. Digital natives, digital immigrants, part II. Do they really think differently? *On the Horizon* 9(6), 1–6. http://nsuworks.nova.edu/cgi/viewcontent.cgi?article=1020&context=innovate [Accessed 10 Aug 2017].

SCONUL Advisory Committee on Information Literacy. 1999. *Information skills in higher education: a SCONUL position paper*. http://www.sconul.ac.uk/groups/information_literacy/seven_pillars.html [Accessed 27 Feb 2011].

SCONUL Working Group on Information Literacy. 2011. *The SCONUL Seven Pillars of Information Literacy: Core Model for Higher Education*. www.sconul.ac.uk/sites/default/files/documents/coremodel.pdf [Accessed 10 Aug 2017].

Selwyn, N. 2009. The digital native: myth and reality. *Aslib Proceedings* 61(4), 364–379.

Sharpe, R. and Beetham, H. 2010. Understanding students' uses of technology for learning: towards creative appropriation. *Rethinking Learning for the Digital Age: How Learners Shape Their Experiences* 85–99.

Sharpe, R., Beetham, H., Benfield, G., DeCicco, E. and Lessner, E. 2009. *Learners Experiences of e-Learning Synthesis Report: Explaining learner differences*. http://jisc.ac.uk/media/documents/programmes/elearningpedagogy/lxp2finalsynthesis.pdf [Accessed 10 Aug 2017].

Street, B. 1998. New literacies in theory and practice: what are the implications for language in education? *Linguistics and Education* 10(1), 1–24.

Tapscott, D. 1998. *Growing up Digital: The Rise of the Net Generation*. New York: McGraw-Hill.

Tay, L. and Diener, E. 2011. Needs and subjective well-being around the world. *Journal of Personality and Social Psychology* 101(2), 354.

Tracy, S. J. 2010. Qualitative quality: eight 'big-tent' criteria for excellent qualitative research. *Qualitative inquiry* 16(10), 837–851.

5

RESEARCHING DIGITAL ENGAGEMENT

In Chapter 1, the core issues addressed in this book were laid out. The ideas of experience and engagement were discussed and the features that characterise the digital university were discussed. How, though, should these ideas be studied in this context? If, for example, student engagement is a contested concept, what does it mean to study it? What might count as evidence of engagement or experience? What is the role of the digital in such work, both as an object of study but also as a way of generating evidence?

This chapter sets out the approach we took to explore these issues. This project has provided us with a rich array of examples that will be used to develop and illustrate the argument in the chapters that follow. In order to give context to these examples, and to make the analysis that was undertaken transparent, we will first discuss the work that was undertaken within the project and the methodology that was used.

The Funding Context

An important point of departure for this discussion involves recognising the policies that influenced the project. The work that was undertaken formed part of a national programme within the UK; the funding for this had been secured in order to create change within the Higher and Further Education sectors. The project was funded by JISC, which, at the time, was the UK's Joint Information Systems Committee, a government-sponsored body responsible for the technological infrastructure of Higher and Further Education. This responsibility included cables that connected institutions to the internet, software deals, digital collections and a remit for training staff about the use of these services. From 2011–2014, JISC sponsored a programme of work on the development of digital literacies, including 12 institutional projects that ran through 2013 and 2014. Following the policies outlined above, the programme overview (now only viewable through the web archive service) opened:

> Many learners enter further and higher education lacking the skills needed to apply digital technologies to education. As 90 per cent of new jobs will require excellent digital skills, improving digital literacy is an essential component of developing employable graduates.
>
> *(JISC 2014)*

The programme as a whole, however, took a broader view of the development of digital literacies, rather than restricting it purely to a deficit model focused on training graduates for industry. The programme built on a scoping review (Beetham, McGill and Littlejohn 2009), which acknowledged economic pressures, uncertain job markets and training demands, but also framed the work in terms of wider social and technological change. Ideas of the networked society, the ubiquity of technology and of digital resources, convergence between work and leisure, the blurring of public/private spaces and the need to manage complex, fragmented identities were also addressed. Academically, the report also raised questions about interdisciplinary forms of work, the growing importance of multimodality, information literacy and emerging forms of digital scholarship.

The challenge of balancing policy imperatives about employability and wider concerns about social and academic development was echoed in many of the projects within the programme, including the one from which this book draws. The project sought to raise questions about the way in which what was at the time a relatively ill-defined concept – digital literacy – was linked to ideas of what it meant to succeed as a student in contemporary Higher Education. The imperative of the programme was development: projects were required to undertake new initiatives such as creating and running new training programmes, or developing recognition schemes. However, the first step for all projects had to consist of what was called a baseline phase, which would provide an evidence base for the work that followed. For our project, this phase ran for the whole first year, forming half of the project; in addition to the practical, institutional impact we wanted to achieve through the project, we also wanted to develop rigorous, scholarly discussions about ideas such as engagement, experience and digital literacies. This scholarship formed the basis for this book, and will be explored in the chapters that follow.

The Research Methodology

What this project required was evidence about how students study successfully, and the role of digital technologies within these practices. Doing this required evidence about the day-to-day, fine-grained practices of students – practices that were unclear, and so could not be captured through closed-item surveys, and which the students themselves might take for granted, making it hard to rely on self-report of the kind commonly requested by open-ended survey questions or in interviews (Gourlay 2010). This required the development of new approaches to generating research evidence.

Research into digital literacies typically takes place within the field of educational technology, which does not have a unifying central theory or approach (Czerniewicz 2010), and which often engages only superficially with theory (Bennett and Oliver 2011). Research typically focuses on issues of satisfaction or effectiveness – a 'what works' agenda, limited to instrumental concerns rather than considering wider interests in understanding phenomena or engaging with issues of equity or justice (Friesen 2009). As Friesen argues, reaching beyond these instrumental concerns requires a different kind of research, something that moves beyond satisfaction surveys or performance tests in order to ask open-ended questions about experiences, meaning and possibilities. Interpretive approaches, especially those working with rich, qualitative data, are well suited to such research agendas. However, these approaches can be challenging when researching how people engage, since studying – in contrast to teaching – is something that people do in a variety of locations and at different times. It would be impractical and invasive for researchers to follow people throughout the day just in case some relevant engagement took place.

Work has been done to develop approaches that can cope with this complexity, however. Earlier JISC-funded work exploring learners' experiences of e-learning (Sharpe *et al.* 2009) confirmed that many projects continued to rely on self-report satisfaction surveys, but noted that various alternatives were beginning to be used. These included the 'interview plus' approach, where artefacts were used to stimulate and ground discussions, and Interpretative Phenomenological Analysis, which asks learners to create narratives about their experiences, and what these meant to them. Jones and Healing (2010) developed what they described as a 'cultural probe' exercise, which involved sending undergraduate students text messages over a period of 24 hours, prompting them to answer specific questions either by recording a video or making notes. This resulted in a data set that described what students were doing, what technologies they were using, where they were doing it, with whom, and how they felt about it. This enabled detailed pictures to be built up about the ways in which they integrated their studies into their life and leisure.

An alternative tradition of work has developed in the field of New Literacy Studies, and this also formed an important point of reference for the project. Here, the focus on social practice resulted in the use of ethnographic methods (e.g. Barton and Hamilton 2012). Although this is ideal for exploring experiences and meanings, it is challenging given the distributed way in which students engage. Recently, this approach has also been challenged for leaving the materiality of contexts relatively unexamined (Gourlay, Hamilton and Lea 2013).

There is a growing interest in sociomaterial perspectives on education, recognising the way in which:

> Human and non-human actors act upon each other throughout the practices of knowledge production.
>
> *(Fenwick, Edwards and Sawchuk 2011:vii)*

This work develops a sociomaterial perspective on education, questioning humanist assumptions that have shaped much social science and educational research. It reveals how engagement with the digital in education is not necessarily a smooth, disembodied, agentive transition from 'novice' to 'expert', but involves instead complex and messy practices that constantly shift and re-emerge, intertwined with unstable settings that act agentively rather than forming a simple backdrop for human action.

This sociomaterial perspective has a relationship with traditions of work such as Actor-Network Theory, or ANT (Latour 2005), in terms of its recognition of nonhuman agency. ANT is a perspective that is ideally suited to the fine-grained study of the ways in which social and material networks give rise to particular effects and identities. However, while ANT's ontology is more inclusive, paying greater attention to materiality and involving a commitment to valuing human and nonhuman actors equally, it has also tended to rely on ethnographic methods. Its conceptual richness was an asset to the project, but methodological work still needed to be done.

A final perspective that helped to bring together these promising but separate elements was digital anthropology. Cultural studies of the digital engaged from an early point with the interrelationships between the digital and virtual. Hine (2000), for example, conducted an early ethnography of cultures that developed on the internet, paying close attention to the ways in which individuals' lives brought together online and offline elements. Her work involved a combination of face-to-face interviews and online participation. More recently, Miller and Horst have argued for a strong commitment to holism, since 'no one lives an entirely digital life and [. . .] no digital media or technologies exist outside of networks that include analogue and other media technologies' (Miller and Horst 2012:16). They draw attention back to materiality as the 'bedrock' for digital anthropology, since digital infrastructure and technology are constituted materially, and the spaces, places and times in which digital practices are enacted shape them in important ways.

The Research Methods

The influences described above framed the work by defining the object of research – students' study practices – as distributed; complex and emergent; bringing together digital, material and social elements; and unfolding moment-to-moment, from day-to-day. The research approach therefore needed to be exploratory, inter-pretive, distributed and longitudinal.

Specific elements from this prior work shaped the approaches that the project eventually adopted. The strong presence of ethnographies in areas such as New Literacy Studies, ANT and digital anthropology fitted well with the commitment to an open and interpretive study. The work in digital anthropology, in particular, showed that ethnographies could take place even where the 'field' defined in relation to digital networks was distributed across physical spaces. This, together with sociomaterial work in education, drew attention to the importance of specific places that shaped practices. Work on students' experiences showed the value of drawing students' attention to their lived practices with prompts, and of interviews that stimulated and grounded discussions through the use of artefacts. Taken together, the project adopted what we described as multimodal longitudinal journaling (Gourlay and Oliver 2016), an ethnographically informed approach that involved a series of interviews with participants who were asked to document their practices over time.

The project as a whole did use other sources of evidence too. Existing student satisfaction survey data was reviewed, although this was quickly dismissed as it lacked detail, elided material details and rarely gave information about practices, only problems. Focus groups were also conducted, and these proved a useful pilot: they allowed a simplified version of the research methods to be tried out and generated a small data set that was useful for orienting the initial interviews with participants. However, the focus in this book will be the series of interviews that was undertaken with participants, and the images, videos and artefacts that they brought along to these.

The study took place at a UK postgraduate institution specialising in edu-cational research. The student body is predominantly mature and postgraduate, the majority of students are female, and many combine their studies with ongoing work and/or family responsibilities. The students come from over 100 countries of origin, meaning that they have experience of a broad range of educational cultures. All this means that, while they may have highly developed digital practices within their own personal or professional settings, they may have little or no experience of many digital technologies that are considered mainstream elements of current Higher Education in the UK.

The focus groups mentioned above were held with four different groups of students: initial teacher education students (studying for a postgraduate certificate in education that would qualify them to teach in the UK), taught Master's degree students, students studying a taught Master's degree entirely at a distance, and doctoral students. Three students from each focus group were invited to take part in the main study, ensuring the diversity of participants, as shown in Table 5.1.

The study was given institutional ethical approval, followed the principle of informed consent, and provided participants with guarantees of anonymity and confidentiality, and the right to opt out at any point. The participants chose their own pseudonyms.

TABLE 5.1 An overview of the participants

Category	Pseudonym	Details
PGCE	Louise	F, 22, British
PGCE	Faith	F, 30, Taiwanese
PGCE	Polly	F, 40, British
MA	Nahid	M, 26, Bangladeshi
MA	Juan	M, 30s, British
MA	Yuki	F, 42, Japanese
Distance	Bokeh	M, 30s, British
Distance	Darren	M, 40s, American
Distance	Lara	F, 40s, Chilean
PhD	Django	F, 39, British
PhD	Sally	F, 41, British
PhD	Frederick	M, 25, German

Generating the Data

The research involved three or four interviews with each participant over 9–12 months. The first interview involved asking students about their educational histories, with a particular focus on the role of technology in their experiences. As part of these initial interviews, each participant was asked to create and explain a drawing of the places and resources that formed part of their studies.

At the end of the interview, each participant was given an iPod Touch and provided with training on how to use it. They were then asked to take about a month to produce a collection of images, videos and textual notes – a multimodal journal – that they felt reflected the 'messy', micro-level, day-to-day practices of studying, with instructions not to include recognisable people in the images, or to take the image of any person without their informed consent. These visual data were intended to ground subsequent interviews in specific examples of practice, avoiding the tendency of stand-alone interviews that rely on self-report to slide into abstraction (Gourlay 2010). Visual methodologies (e.g. Pink 2013, Rose 2013) were used for several reasons. First, as the focus of the project was on the minutiae of day-to-day unfolding practice, it was felt that standard 'account' interviews were not likely to be suitable in terms of revealing practices at any level of granularity – instead, they were more likely to lead to further abstraction and generalisation if students were asked to described their engagement in general terms via verbal description and recall alone. We required them to capture images to use as heuristics and prompts for discussion, in order to attempt to anchor the interview in the detail of the day-to-day, particularly in relation to aspects of engagement which do not normally make the 'headlines' when student engagement is being discussed, elements of practice which may be disregarded as mundane, inconsequential or simply part of supposedly transparent and unproblematic communication processes. Images seemed well suited for documenting these subtle, private and small-scale moments of emergent practice. Second, a visual approach seemed suitable for a project which was focused on the nonhuman and supposedly inert artefacts of practice, as a focus on these through images would lead to greater attention being paid to the objects themselves. Third, it was felt that the use of photography and video would be more engaging and appear less onerous to the participants than a written journal. Finally, the students took their own images and selected which ones to discuss in the interviews, which allowed us to explore their engagement more closely from their own point of view.

The participants took responsibility for curating these data, deciding which to bring along to the next interview and what to say about them. As well as these digital data, participants brought along material artefacts that were important to them, such as books, notebooks, highlighter pens, Post-it notes, folders, printed papers and completed surveys. The second and subsequent interviews consisted of the participants presenting their journal data to the interviewer, and then discussing them.

At the end of each interview, which typically lasted over an hour, participants were asked whether they remained willing to participate in the project and whether they thought they might still have new points to make in the next phase of journaling work. They were then set a more focused task for the following month, allowing richer and more detailed accounts to be developed of the material, spatial and temporal elements of their everyday practices. These later tasks included focusing on the ways in which they made use of the institutional infrastructure – for example, things like the library, or the course virtual learning environment (VLE) – and their textual practices (such as using source texts or data sets, or producing assessed work such as essays, chapters or dissertations). As the interviews progressed, participants provided increasingly structured and thoughtful commentaries on the data they presented, with some students creating presentations, using PowerPoint or Prezi, that brought together images with explanatory texts, or grouped images into themes that they saw as important in explaining their experiences.

All the interviews were transcribed, and the digital data (images, notes, etc.) brought to each session were associated with the relevant transcripts. In addition, any material artefacts brought along to the sessions (such as books, papers and so on) were photographed during the interview, or a video was taken while the participant explained them. The same was done for drawings made during the interviews, such as the drawing of places and resources in the first interview. These were also associated with the relevant transcripts to complete the data set.

Interpreting the Data

The process of interpreting the data consisted of a series of steps. The first was a simple descriptive reading, which in itself allowed some useful conclusions to be drawn. For example, this made it clear that there were markedly different experiences of the same institutional infrastructure across the groups of participants. PGCE students, for example, looked for readings through the digitised reading lists on their VLE, whereas doctoral students searched on specialist library databases and Google Scholar. It also allowed us to identify over 30 different devices and pieces of software that our students were using, and how the use of these varied by personal circumstance and subject studied. For example, students with jobs kept separate email services for work, personal use and studying; those studying geography education thought GPS was important whereas those studying (say) philosophy made no mention of this.

This initial descriptive review was mainly useful for challenging generalisations, such as assumptions about the stability of digital literacies or the nature of student engagement. (Illustrations of this kind of critique were referred to in Chapters 3 and 4.) This in itself was useful, particularly in areas such as educational technology where discussions and policy have been developed without reference to an evidence base. However, in order to move beyond description, a thematic analysis was undertaken. This clustered together data that related to common experiences or issues. This was useful, for example, in drawing attention to the way students were managing their uses of space and time, and in identifying common orientations towards the use of technology. (These are topics that will be discussed further in Chapters 8 and 6, respectively.)

A third pass through the data was then undertaken, relating the emergent themes to foundational concepts from areas of work such as New Literacy Studies, academic literacies, ANT and sociomateriality. This allowed, for example, the thematic orientation of 'coping' to be related to wider literature about the concept of educational resilience, allowing the connection and development of previously separate theories, as shown in Chapter 9.

Conclusions

Ideas such as engagement and experience, or discussions about topics such as digital literacy, have been shaped by wider policies and debates about the relationship between universities and society. But these debates need not determine how we think about students, their needs or their activities, as the project outlined here shows. Alongside the developmental agenda that justified the funding, it was possible to develop a scholarly and theorised account of how our students engaged with their studies, and of the diversity of their experiences. This involved the development of new ways of generating and interpreting evidence about their ongoing, day-to-day study practices, which made it possible to understand students' experiences in new ways and think through ways in which these could be made more equitable rather than merely considering instrumental concerns about efficiency or effectiveness.

The next chapter will show how this approach allowed mainstream claims about 'the digital' in Higher Education to be critiqued and rethought, contrasting the claims of advocates with the experiences reported by the students who participated in this project. It offers an alternative and more fluid unit of analysis than the frameworks or categories critiqued earlier in this book, focusing instead on the shifting and fluid nature of student *orientations* to their engagement with the digital.

References

Barton, D. and Hamilton, M. 2012. *Local Literacies: A Study of Reading and Writing in One Community*. London: Routledge.

Bennett, S. and Oliver, M. 2011. Talking back to theory: the missed opportunities in learning technology research. *Research in Learning Technology* 19(3), 179–189.

Beetham, H., McGill, L. and Littlejohn, A. 2009. *Thriving in the 21st Century: Learning Literacies for the Digital Age (LLiDA Project)*. Glasgow: The Caledonian Academy, Glasgow Caledonian University. www.caledonianacademy.net/spaces/LLiDA/uploads/Main/LLiDAreportJune09.pdf [Accessed 10 Aug 2017].

Czerniewicz, L. 2010. Educational technology: mapping the terrain with Bernstein as cartographer. *Journal of Computer Assisted Learning* 26(6), 523–534.

Fenwick, T., Edwards, R. and Sawchuk, P. 2011. *Emerging Approaches to Educational Research: Tracing the Sociomaterial*. London: Routledge.

Friesen, N. 2009. *Rethinking E-learning Research*. New York: Peter Lang.

Gourlay, L. 2010. Multimodality, visual methodologies and higher education. In M. Savin-Baden and C. Howell Major (Eds.), *New Approaches to Qualitative Research: Wisdom and Uncertainty*. London: Routledge, 80–88.

Gourlay, L. and Oliver, M. 2016. Multimodal longitudinal journaling. In C. Haythornthwaite, R. Andrews, J. Fransman and E. Meyers (Eds.), *The SAGE Handbook of E-learning Research*. London: SAGE, 291–312.

Gourlay, L., Hamilton, M. and Lea, M. 2013. Textual practices in the new media landscape: messing with digital literacies. *Research in Learning Technologies* 21(1), 1–13.

Hine, C. 2000. *Virtual Ethnography*. London: SAGE.

JISC 2014. *Developing digital literacies programme website*. http://webarchive.nationalarchives.gov.uk/20140703053208/http://www.jisc.ac.uk/whatwedo/programmes/elearning/developingdigitalliteracies [Accessed 10 Aug 2017].

Jones, C. and Healing, G. 2010. Networks and locations for student learning. *Learning, Media and Technology* 35(4), 369–385.

Latour, B. 2005. *Reassembling the Social: An Introduction to Actor-Network-Theory*. Oxford: Oxford University Press.

Miller, D. and Horst, H. 2012. The digital and the human: a prospectus for digital anthropology. In H. Horst and D. Miller (Eds.), *Digital Anthropology*. London: Berg, 3–35.

Pink, S. 2013. *Doing Visual Ethnography* (3rd Ed.). London: SAGE.

Rose, G. 2013. *Visual Methodologies: An Introduction to Researching with Visual Materials* (3rd Ed.). London: SAGE.

Sharpe, R., Beetham, H., Benfield, G., DeCicco, E. and Lessner, E. 2009. *Learners' experiences of e-learning synthesis report: explaining learner differences*. http://jisc.ac.uk/media/documents/programmes/elearningpedagogy/lxp2finalsynthesis.pdf [Accessed 10 Aug 2017].

6

ENTANGLEMENTS WITH THE DIGITAL

Being critical about frameworks and taxonomies clears the ground for new ways of thinking about students' experiences. However, it also sweeps away superficially convenient ways of making claims about them.

This chapter explores what kinds of conclusions can be drawn about students' patterns of engagement, once such fixed forms of framing have been set aside. It opens with a methodological discussion, looking at the consequences of moving away from frameworks. Next, it presents an approach that remains consistent with the situated, emergent accounts discussed above. Finally, it illustrates this approach by discussing examples of students' engagements with digital and material devices, as well as with people, during the course of their studies. These are characterised as orientations towards study, drawing on data and analysis from the project described in the previous chapter.

After Frameworks: Rethinking the Unit of Analysis

Part of the appeal of frameworks is the clarity they seem to bring to analysis. They offer ways of sorting things out, and this constructs a particular account of the world that makes it amenable to analysis (Bowker and Star 1999). In doing so, however, they can obscure the mess of day-to-day differences and variation, providing an appealing illusion of consistency and conformity. As Bowker and Star argue, such apparent clarity can hide the politics behind the scheme: classifying things is a form of social practice, one that rests on the assumptions and conventions of the people who developed the classification scheme, and which is further shaped by the world view of those doing the classification. As such, classification can normalise particular points of view, and can entrench political inequality within material cultures. Bowker and Star provide, as examples of this, the way in which internationally standardised medical classifications reflect the concerns of colonial powers who sought to control the spread of tropical diseases to their own shores, and the ways in which surveys of ethnicity can require people to classify themselves as conforming to a racial type with which they may not fully identify.

The reason that such schemes remain so appealing is precisely because they are simplifications: they make the work of classifying things appear less problematic. For example, if Prensky's original formulation (Prensky 2001) of 'digital natives' had proved reliable, rather than being systematically undermined by subsequent studies of people and their practices (e.g. Bennett, Maton and Kervin 2008), then all that would be required to classify someone as being 'digitally literate' (or not) would be to know whether they were born before or after 1985.

The appeal of such a neat, binary outcome from something as straightforward as knowing a date of birth avoids all the ambiguity of the situation – but it also destroys its complexity. Across the social sciences, there has been a wide movement away from such reductionist approaches, and instead towards accounts that value more holistic, more situated explanations. Matusov (2007) discusses the methodological developments that took place in order to provide more holistic, inclusive accounts of learners and their experiences, expanding the 'unit of analysis' to include social as well as individual explanations. The same kind of movement can be seen in related fields such as human–computer interaction (Grudin 1990), where the notion of the computer 'reaching out' into the social has led to widespread studies of uses of technology in settings such as workplaces, rather than a reliance on lab-based experiments. Such work has made increasing use of concepts such as 'ecologies' to make sense of the ways people use technology (e.g. Nardi 1996, Luckin 2010). Such work has turned, increasingly, towards ethnomethodological approaches (e.g. Garfinkel 1967), which enable research to focus on the everyday, 'micro' practices that might otherwise be missed.

As noted in Chapter 5, this same move towards situatedness, complexity and emergence can also be seen in research exploring students' experiences. The review by Sharpe *et al.* of methodologies used to investigate students' experience of digital engagement showed an initial dominance of self-report satisfaction surveys (Sharpe *et al.* 2009). These remove the ambiguity of classification from the analyst to the participant, who has to reduce the richness and complexity of their lives into the best available option selected from a closed list, occasionally supplemented by a short 'other' box allowing some free text to be entered. However, Sharpe *et al.* noted how these approaches were increasingly complemented by alternatives that focused on culture and context. These involved forms of qualitative data, such as the discussions of students' artefacts in the 'interview plus' approach; or students' narrative accounts about their experiences and what these meant to them, as used in Interpretive Phenomenological Analysis (Sharpe *et al.* 2009). Although many of these approaches involve working with qualitative data, quantitative approaches also featured. For example, Jones and Healing (2010) explored patterns of study using a cultural probe exercise. This involved sending undergraduate students

SMS messages throughout a day, prompting them to respond either through video or in a notebook. Rather than generating narratives for interpretation, this approach created descriptive, categorical data about what students did, using what technologies, where, with whom, and how they felt about it. Such patterns might be complemented by qualitative data, but could also be analysed in their own right.

In all of these arenas, the turn from closed systems of classification towards more open and exploratory approaches allowed new kinds of question to be asked. Friesen (2009) argues that over the last decade, e-learning research has explored a very narrow range of questions. Experiments and surveys have dominated the field, being used to answer questions of efficiency, and simplistic binary questions about what works (and by implication, what does not). However, he argues, such studies have done little to reveal what such uses of technology might mean to people, or what the political consequences of these technologies might be, in terms of changing the balance of power that people experience. Asking these kinds of questions requires a different approach to research.

Networks and Emergence

According to Latour, there is a tendency within social science to present phenomena as matters of fact.

> When social scientists add the adjective 'social' to some phenomenon, they designate a stabilized state of affairs, a bundle of ties that, later, may be mobilized to account for some other phenomenon.
>
> *(Latour 2005:1)*

However, rather than assuming such stability, research that adopts a networked perspective treats such situations as matters of *concern*: the relative stability of a 'fact' is part of what needs to be explained, rather than something that can be taken for granted (Latour 2005:120). From this perspective, accounting for phenomena involves tracing the ties needed to create a successful 'assemblage' – or else to identify which ties were unsuccessful and prevented such an assemblage from stabilising. This 'heterogeneous engineering' (Law 1992) involves explaining the way in which different people and things have been brought together to enable something to happen. Understanding these situations involves explaining how these assemblages have emerged and how they have persisted.

However, one issue with a network-based analysis is that there are rarely clear boundaries. Connections can always be traced further, drawing in new elements at each step (Latour 1999). The consequence of this is that the analyst must take a decision about where to cut the network, so that it appears bounded and coherent – and from a practical point of view, so that it is manageable to study it. The taxonomic approaches discussed earlier, such as 'digital natives' or 'engagement styles', typically make such cuts around an individual, treating them as if they were self-contained and free-floating, unaffected by any context they might find themselves in, as argued in earlier chapters. One contrasting alternative is to reach out, tracing the network to see how far it reaches. This can provide surprising insights. For example, Starosielski has focused her analysis on 'undersea cables, the infrastructures that currently support over 95 per cent of transoceanic internet traffic and transmit much global visual culture' (Starosielski 2012:39). Such material infrastructure is commonly hidden (e.g. by burying it) or ignored (e.g. becoming invisible through repeated use), and appears to have little relevance to the day-to-day experience of students' lives. This apparent irrelevance, in spite of the volume of data individual learners might access using these cables, arises because when the infrastructure works it operates as a 'black box' (Latour 2005:202), hiding its internal workings from everyday users. The success of 'black boxing' these networks means that, for an analysis of specific examples of successful day-to-day use, these elements can be cut from the analysis of the network and taken for granted. (They will, however, be brought back into focus in the analysis in Chapter 9.)

Other material elements, however, must remain in focus if we are to understand learners' patterns of engagement. Hayles (2004) has argued that discussions of 'virtuality' and of the digital often overlook physical components that are necessary to what is going on. As an example, she argues that discussions of information frequently take place as if information was insubstantial, when information patterns are in fact always instantiated as material objects.

> The digital computer is not, strictly speaking, entirely digital. At the most basic level of the computer are electronic polarities, which are related to the bit stream through the analogue correspondence of morphological resemblance. Once the bit stream is formed, it operates as digital code. Analogue resemblance typically reappears at the top level of the screenic image, for example, in the desktop icon of a trash barrel. Thus digital computers have an Oreo cookie–like structure with an analogue bottom, a frothy digital middle, and an analogue top.
>
> *(Hayles 2004:75)*

In this context, Hayles' analysis draws attention to the ways in which students' texts are created, stored, accessed and engaged with. (Texts here are understood broadly, including multimodal semiotic resources as well as conventional written texts.) Such acts of finding, reading and writing specifically academic texts are central to understanding what it means to study in Higher Education (Gourlay, Oliver and Lanclos 2015). From a sociomaterial perspective, it is important to differentiate between different versions of the text, and how these are created, destroyed or turned into each other – whether, for example, they exist in print, on memory sticks, on servers or displayed on screens. This analysis requires close attention to how imprints might be created and modified – for example, whether reading involves accessing definitive copies stored on a publisher's servers, using pens to mark up a printed version, or creating a digital text of an interview by listening to the recording and typing in what is heard.

Studying Orientations

This analysis of the emergence and stabilisation of heterogeneous networks has explanatory power, but does not lend itself to normative claims. It might explain how a student succeeds or fails, but this account cannot in itself support claims that this particular student will ever act in the same way again. They might find themselves in situations where different people or resources are available to them, or they might learn some new way to deal with similar situations, or the demands placed on them might change over time. Similarly, the analysis cannot predict how other students might react in similar circumstances. What it can do, however, is characterise styles of response. When analysing the data set created during the project described in Chapter 5, one of the first steps in making sense of students' experiences was to identify vignettes from the interviews.

Curation

Yuki was a female in her 40s who had travelled from Japan to study an MA. In her interviews, she described how her iPad had become central to the way she studied. From her first interview, for example, she described how she used it to create digital recordings of lectures.

> For example, when I attend a lecture or a session I always record the session, and it's after the session, but sometimes I listen to the lecture again to confirm my knowledge or reflect the session . . . when I, for example, we're writing an essay and I have to . . . confirm what the lecturer said, I could confirm with the recording data.
>
> *(Yuki Interview 1)*

There were some digital tasks that she still could not do with the iPad, such as sustained writing. For these tasks, she either used her laptop or a desktop computer within the institution. However, her extensive use of the iPad enabled her to move from place to place, so that she could study in a range of different settings.

> For me the most important thing is portability, because I use technologies, ICT, everywhere I go, anywhere I go.
>
> *(Yuki Interview 1)*

One interesting example of this was the way in which she created digital versions of print books. She brought to the interview a series of pictures of pieces of second-hand academic books that she had bought. She explained that she wanted to use her iPad to store digital copies of the academic texts she thought she might use when writing her assignments. Some of these were available under institutional licenses; she was able to download these directly onto the iPad. Others were not, and these were the books that she bought copies of. She then microwaved the books, melting the glue in the spine, and took the pages out. She fed these loose pages through a high-speed scanner, creating a digital copy of the book in PDF format. She then loaded these PDFs onto the iPad.

She also brought along the image shown in Figure 6.1. She explained:

> Sometimes I read in the bathroom. This place is very good to concentrate to my reading. [Interviewer: Oh, that's your iPad there, isn't it, on the bath? And you've told me before that you've got a special bag . . . ?] Oh yes, I need a Ziploc plastic bag to cover the iPad.
>
> *(Yuki Interview 3)*

Yuki's account illustrates several important themes. The way in which she scanned books to create digital versions stored on her iPad illustrates the kind of material analysis of text creation that Hayles (2004) discusses, showing how material texts were destroyed and recreated, in order to use another material technology – a scanner – to create a digital copy, which was then stored on her iPad. This was

FIGURE 6.1   Yuki's iPad

important because of the value she placed on portability – adding the digital text to the iPad did nothing to increase the weight or volume of material she had to carry, whereas the physical book would have done. The iPad enabled her to feel 'less bound by place' (Yuki, presentation data for interview 3), an expression that suggests newfound freedom.

This can be understood from the perspective of mobilities developed by Edwards, Tracy and Jordan (2011) – a perspective that will be explored in greater depth in Chapter 7. Edwards *et al.* argue that:

> Rather than starting analysis from a space out of which objects move, this approach aims to map mobilities and the ways in which spaces are moored, bounded and stabilised for the moment, and the specific (im) mobilities associated with such moorings. We might take such spaces for granted – as, for instance, universities – but a mobilities analysis would examine the ways in which such spaces are enacted and become sedimented across time.
>
> *(Edwards, Tracy and Jordan 2011:223)*

From their perspective, the way Yuki studied became more mobile with respect to space, allowing her to study in the library, the park or even her bath. However, this comes at a price: she has become less mobile with respect to the devices she relies upon when studying. The stability of her study practice depends on the availability of her iPad; this becomes a point of mooring, a sedimented part of her reading and writing practices. From the perspective of networked analyses described above, the studying was not the same in each location: the elements that she assembled varied, depending on whether she was in the library, the park or the bath; however, one of the consistent elements across the fluidity of these networks was her iPad.

Overall, Yuki's ability to create successful conditions for studying in a range of settings was taken as a mark of fluency. What characterised this fluency was the way that she brought together diverse multimodal texts (recordings, written texts, images) and managed them using the iPad, so that she could continue to study them in a variety of different places. These practices of managing texts in order to support her studies can be understood as a form of curation. Potter (2012:5) explains that 'curating suggests not just writing or producing but also *collecting, distributing, assembling, disassembling,* and *moving* media artifacts and content', and further describes it as 'active, agentive and evaluative' (174). Here, Yuki has created various multimodal texts, including the sound recordings of lectures and the PDF version of books. She has collected these on her iPad, and then assembled them as resources in support of her academic writing. Her particular approach to this was distinctive and extensive – but many participants described similar practices, often involving the management of PDF texts on memory sticks or cloud drives in preparation for writing essays.

Combat

Sally was a doctoral student, a female in her 40s from the UK, whose programme of study spanned two institutions. Her interviews showed that she was a capable and successful user of technology, with decades of professional and personal experience to draw on. However, the ways in which she talked about technology were quite different from those of Yuki, in that they exhibited a sense of threat or risk. For example:

> I was like bullied into it by people saying, oh, you'll be left behind if you don't use Facebook. So yes, that was when I got into it, so . . . And then . . . so now I would say Facebook, I'm not the most . . . [. . .] I'm a bit uncomfortable about the whole kind of like Big Brother aspect.
>
> *(Sally Interview 1)*

There are two important elements to the way in which she talks about this sense of threat. The first was that she demonstrated a deep understanding of the ways in which these services used algorithms to work out things about her – something that she felt impinged on her privacy. The second related point was that she did not feel she was in control about what personal information was made available to different audiences, but she wanted to be.

> I feel like, also that Google is equally watching you. You know, they're all watching you, they're all trying to sell you things, and the thing is not, I don't so much mind being bombarded with advertising as I mind having things put about me on things like Facebook that I don't want. You know, I don't want my friends to spy on me, I don't want my friends to know what I listen to on YouTube.
>
> *(Sally Interview 1)*

She made frequent use of words such as 'spy'; in the focus group that preceded the journaling study, she said about her phone that 'I've got a spy in my bag' (Sally, doctoral focus group).

Unlike Yuki's account, in which the technology that she used to curate materials is all but invisible, Sally's accounts foreground it. It is not simply a tool to be used, but something that she experiences as agentive, not completely under her control, and not always to be trusted. Other participants, too, spoke about technologies that were not entirely under their control – for example, because versions of software had changed and they could no longer make it do what they wanted, but more commonly because the algorithms hidden from users meant that technologies could act in ways that the user did not understand and perhaps did not expect, and had to learn how to deal with.

This kind of experience echoes the theoretical discussion in Chapter 2 about the relative agency of people and technology – a concern that will be developed further in Chapter 7.

Coping

Faith was a Taiwanese student, pursuing an initial teacher education course (a PGCE) to qualify to teach in the UK. In her interviews, she talked about several technologies that were distinctive to the practices of teaching in schools. However, one particularly vivid incident in her account concerned a very mundane technology: a printer. Faith brought a photograph of the printer along to the interview (Figure 6.2).

She explained the image as follows:

> In my school, I . . . we had . . . our staff room was equipped . . . one, two, three, four, five, six, seven . . . seven computers now we can use and only one of them attached with a printer. So, actually we've got six PGCE students over there, so it's, kind of, everybody wants to get to that computer where you can use the printer. [. . .] So, six student teachers tried to use other computer. So, it, kind of, sometimes feels a bit crowded. And when the school staff want to use it, well, okay, it seems like we are the invaders, intruders?
>
> *(Faith Interview 2)*

Faith was perfectly capable of using a printer from a technical point of view. What she struggled with was the wider environment – the social elements of this network – in which the printer was located. The politics of the staff room, and, in particular, the marginal status of the students who were at the school on training placements, prevented her from printing off the materials that she needed for the lessons she had to teach. For Faith, this was an important site of professional learning. She knew how to use the technologies; what she did not know was how

FIGURE 6.2 Faith's printer

to secure access to them in a reliable way. In this case, she concluded that she would not be given the access she needed in time for the lesson she had to teach, so she abandoned that printer and set off to find another one elsewhere in the school.

> Yes, so in the end I found actually I can also use the printer from the library in the school.
>
> *(Faith Interview 2)*

What characterises Faith's account is the sense in which her use of technology was precarious; she could not simply use it (as she eventually did in the example above) or even struggle with the situation until she could find a way to work with it (as Sally had in her earlier example), but instead had to give up and constitute a slightly different network instead – one in which there was less competition for a comparable technical network.

Various students struggled to make technology do what they wanted. Louise, for example, described a task that required her to share printed notes with peers:

> I wrote a page up on the computers so that my peers could read it, but then I essentially kind of abandoned it and went back to my handwriting [. . .] because when I'm writing notes I'll do sort of like arrows and I'll show what the links are that I'm making in my head.
>
> *(Louise Interview 4)*

This was something that she could not find a way to do in Word. Students would eventually find some alternative way to achieve what they were trying to do – but this often involved abandoning some part of the network, and looking for some other technology, people, place or time to work with instead. As Pollock (2005) has argued, such 'work-arounds' are widespread and are important in understanding the relationships between the logics of a technology and the logics of human work, drawing attention to the contingencies of such 'networks in place'. This illustrates how the assemblages that support study practices are fluid and emergent, an idea that will be explored further in Chapter 7.

Avoiding Types

Chapter 4 drew attention to the risks of slipping from the analysis of situated cases into the development of normative types as some kind of framework. To avoid such a slip here, it is important to emphasise that the orientations presented above do not constitute 'types' of students. There are two lines of argument that are important to foreground in order to explain this.

First, the three orientations presented here were the result of thematic analysis – close reading of the data set to identify 'emergent codes', ideas that emerged as patterns were discerned in the data set. However, discernment is an interpretive act.

These were patterns that we, as the researchers, identified as useful in making sense of the rich data we were analysing. As with all interpretive work, other readings would have been possible, and other readers may well discern other patterns within the data. This does not invalidate our reading and analysis, but it does draw attention to the fact that other orientations – as well as themes of completely different kinds – could well be identified by other researchers or by further analytical work. These orientations are informative, but they are not exhaustive.

Second, these orientations are not exclusive. The examples used above illustrate particular patterns of relationship in vivid ways, but the fact that a student showed a particular orientation in one element of their practice should not be understood to mean that this was the only way in which they were able to relate to technology, nor was it necessarily even the dominant way; no data were collected about the prevalence of these experiences, nor is it even clear what might constitute a sensible way to measure something as interpretively complex as the prevalence of an orientation. To avoid any doubt about the complexity and diversity of students' experiences, each individual will be revisited briefly in turn, to illustrate that these cannot be understood as categories of student.

Yuki

In the example above, Yuki's experience was characterised as a curating orientation. Other parts of her account, however, show very different experiences. For example, Yuki described the struggles she faced understanding lectures, partly as a result of English not being her first language. In addition to taking notes, she created digital records so that she could check that she had understood things correctly.

> When I attend a lecture or a session I always record the session, and it's after the session, but sometimes I listen to the lecture again to confirm my knowledge or reflect on the session. [Interviewer: do you often listen again, or just sometimes?] Not so often, but when I, for example, we're writing an essay and I have to [. . .] confirm what the lecturer said, I could confirm with the recording data.
>
> *(Yuki Interview 1)*

Similarly, when talking about technology use in her professional context, she describes how she had to manage medical data for hundreds of patients.

> For example, surgical data we have to manage, so we wanted to use some useful device, and the first database I tried to make was on Excel, and it was Windows 95, might be. I did try the DOS computer, the previous one, yes, but failed because it was so restricted, it had restricted performance.
>
> *(Yuki Interview 1)*

Although this is a story that is about eventual success, the narrative shows how early attempts failed. In her academic work, she also described how she had stopped using e-books.

> There are so many types of e-books and these e-books provided by the library or Bloomsbury are not so good I think. I cannot extend the font on that, and I cannot highlight or write something. I prefer PDFs or physical books.
>
> *(Yuki Interview 2)*

In both cases, Yuki coped by abandoning a part of the initial assemblage, and then finding a more successful workaround.

Sally

While many of Sally's stories portrayed technology as having agency, there were also examples that clearly demonstrated the extent of her own agency. In some of these, she seemed to surprise herself with what she was able to achieve, as with her account of curating her personal music files.

> Yesterday I had a breakthrough. I got my old iTunes account – this is really old – enabled through this iPod. I used the cloud. I never used the cloud before. I got my previously purchased music to download. Wow!
>
> *(Sally Interview 2)*

Sally also spoke about 'another example of me trying to manage my public profile and failing' (Sally Interview 2) – something that goes beyond the examples of struggling but coping that many of the participants in this study shared. This example involved an alumni magazine being sent to her flat, when she had requested that it be sent to her parents' house instead.

> They must have been data-sharing with the colleges to update their database. [. . .] There's me trying to manage my addresses and what gets sent where and people are just sharing data behind your back, you know, in a way that you're not even in control of and then it's like, now all my neighbours will know that I went to Cambridge University and like, actually it's none of their business and I don't want them to know that.
>
> *(Sally Interview 2)*

Unable to control the way in which the alumni office was using her data, she cancelled the subscription instead.

Faith

Faith's difficulties in printing resources before lessons underplay the expertise she had developed in using technologies for teaching. She described, for example, the way that she curated resources for her maths lessons.

> It's another website that I found really useful. [. . .] There are a lot of nice, good teachers, they have provided some useful resources over there, so it's a good place to go and sometimes if you don't have any inspiration about anything, just go there and see what people have done so far, and then you can just, yes, modify things and then make it into your own thing.
>
> *(Faith Interview 3)*

The resources she was able to use after finding them on this site varied considerably, including PDF worksheets, images, self-contained digital games and presentations in PowerPoint. Faith also described trying out different kinds of interactive whiteboards, so that when she encountered a new one that she was unfamiliar with, she would be better prepared to make it do what she wanted.

> In those two schools that I had, they all have interactive whiteboards, but they have different whiteboards. [. . .] And then later on, my new school, I have another type of board [. . .] and they don't compatible with each other, which is a shame.
>
> *(Faith Interview 4)*

> I try to use both things when I was in the school because I was thinking it would be nice to just learn how to use those interactive whiteboards. [Interviewer: so, the more experience you have with using different types of whiteboards, the easier it is when you confront a new one?] Yes, you are right, yes.
>
> *(Faith Interview 4)*

Here, Faith illustrates how experiences that might be understood as a kind of 'combat' can shift over time, as she learned new ways to work with these technologies through the series of challenges she lined up for herself.

Conclusions

Students' relationships with technology are complex, evolving and constantly renegotiated. The temptation offered by frameworks is to neaten this messiness by categorising people and things. The challenge for this work was to develop a way of describing participants' experiences that would make them comprehensible without reducing their richness. Theoretically, this involved the idea that qualities emerge from the ways in which specific networks are configured. Rather than assuming that our students are fixed and stable entities, we worked with the idea that they adapt, respond to and also shape the situations in which they find themselves. As a result, taxonomic labels – such as 'digital native' - must be avoided, as they suggest a misleading kind of fixity.

Instead, the orientations offered here explore the complex interplays of agency, including struggles of power between different people and things. Reflecting back to the discussions of agency in Chapter 2, this analysis neither positions learners nor technologies as the sole determining influence of students' engagement. Instead, it is the complex interplay of different agencies that gives rise to particular orientations, which are understood as sociomaterial practices. Yuki was not simply a curator, although she curated learning materials in sophisticated ways; at other moments, she struggled and even failed, and none of these moments define her categorically. Similarly, Sally and Faith – and indeed all of the participants – showed a rich array of experiences, influenced but not simplistically determined by the people and things with which they worked.

Having framed students' engagements with the digital in this emergent way, in the next chapter we will take a closer look at an aspect of student engagement which this chapter has introduced – the central and agentive role of nonhuman actors, materiality and embodiment in practices.

References

Bennett, S., Maton, K. and Kervin, L. 2008. The 'digital natives' debate: a critical review of the evidence. *British Journal of Educational Technology* 39(5), 775–786.

Bowker, G. and Star, S. 1999. *Sorting Things Out: Classification and its Consequences.* Cambridge, MA: MIT Press.

Edwards, R., Tracy, F. and Jordan, K. 2011. Mobilities, moorings and boundary marking in developing semantic technologies in educational practices. *Research in Learning Technology* 19(3), 219–232.

Friesen, N. 2009. *Rethinking E-learning Research.* New York: Peter Lang.

Garfinkel, H. 1967. *Studies in Ethnomethodology.* New Jersey: Prentice-Hall.

Gourlay, L., Oliver, M. and Lanclos, D. 2015. Sociomaterial texts, spaces and devices: questioning 'digital dualism' in library and study practices. *Higher Education Quarterly* 69(3), 263–278.

Grudin, J. 1990. The computer reaches out: the historical continuity of interface design. In *Proceedings of the SIGCHI Conference on Human Factors in Computing Systems.* New York: ACM, 261–268.

Hayles, N. K. 2004. Print is flat, code is deep: the importance of media-specific analysis. *Poetics Today* 25(1), 67–90.

Jones, C. and Healing, G. 2010. Networks and locations for student learning. *Learning, Media and Technology* 35(4), 369–385.

Latour, B. 1999. On recalling ANT. *The Sociological Review* 47(1), 15–25.

Latour, B. 2005. *Reassembling the Social: An Introduction to Actor-Network-Theory.* Oxford: Oxford University Press.

Law, J. 1992. Notes on the theory of the actor-network: ordering, strategy, and hetero-geneity. *Systemic Practice and Action Research* 5(4), 379–393.

Luckin, R. 2010. *Re-designing Learning Contexts: Technology-Rich, Learner-Centred Ecologies.* London: Routledge.

Matusov, E. 2007. In Search of the 'Appropriate' Unit of Analysis for Sociocultural Research. *Culture & Psychology* 13(3), 307–333.

Nardi, B. 1996. *Context and Consciousness: Activity Theory and Human–Computer Interaction.* Cambridge, MA: MIT Press.

Pollock, N. (2005) When is a work-around? Conflict and negotiation in computer systems development. *Science, Technology, & Human Values* 30(4), 496–514.

Potter, J. 2012. *Digital Media and Learner Identity: The New Curatorship.* Basingstoke: Palgrave Macmillan.

Prensky, M. 2001. Digital natives, digital immigrants. *On the Horizon* 9(5), 1–6.

Sharpe, R., Beetham, H., Benfield, G., DeCicco, E. and Lessner, E. 2009. *Learners experiences of e-learning synthesis report: explaining learner differences.* http://jisc.ac.uk/media/documents/programmes/elearningpedagogy/lxp2finalsynthesis.pdf [Accessed 10 Aug 2017].

Starosielski, N. 2012. 'Warning: do not dig': negotiating the visibility of critical infra-structures. *Journal of Visual Culture* 11(1), 38–57.

7

NONHUMAN ACTORS, MATERIALITY AND EMBODIMENT

The previous chapters have sought to resituate our understanding of student engagement with the digital in various ways. Chapter 4 examined how student engagement is described in mainstream educational research and policy, presenting a challenge to notions of skills frameworks and typologies of students. Chapter 6 proposed the alternative notion of *orientations* to take account of student engagement in terms of the digital. This chapter will continue the focus on practices, by looking in more detail at agency, and challenging some of the 'common-sense' assumptions made about devices, material objects and embodiment.

Beyond 'Tools'

As we have seen, conventional perspectives on both digital engagement and meaning-making practices tend to place the individual student – the human – at the centre of the model. Engagement is seen to flow purely from the decision-making and actions of that individual. In this view, devices and artefacts are seen as tools which are directed by the will of the user. The social and material settings of engagement are contexts against which practices take place. In this chapter, we will challenge these assumptions and propose an alternative account of agency, drawing on Actor-Network Theory (e.g. Latour 2005). This perspective changes how we see material objects and settings, viewing them not as inert tools and contexts, but as nonhuman actors. This shift leads us from a social model (based on the insights of New Literacy Studies or NLS) to a *sociomaterial* model which seeks to include the material in how we conceive of agency. Scholars working in NLS incorporated this perspective into their work in order to extend the theoretical purchase offered by a 'socially situated' model (e.g. Clarke 2002, Lankshear and Knobel 2008, Hamilton 2011). In a joint paper (Gourlay, Hamilton and Lea 2013), this proposed move was explored in detail, where it was argued that that NLS has been relatively slow to address the digital, with some notable exceptions (e.g.Goodfellow and Lea 2007, Lea 2007, Lea and Jones 2011, Williams 2009, Goodfellow and Lea 2013), and despite the insights of NLS, its roots in applied linguistics and social semiotics may lead to a tendency to 'bracket off' materiality with an overemphasis on language and representation.

> Removing the agency of texts and tools in formalising movements risks romanticising the practices as well as the humans in them; focusing uniquely on the texts and tools lapses into naïve formalism or techno-centrism.
>
> *(Leander and Lovvorn 2006:301)*

Latour (2005) makes the point that in mainstream social science, objects are not seen as part of 'the social', which is seen as a primarily human domain. He proposes that objects should be seen as social actors and makes the distinction between two types – *intermediaries* and *mediators*. He defines an intermediary as '. . . what transports meaning or force without transformation: defining its inputs is enough to define its outputs' (2005:39). In contrast, mediators '. . . transform, translate, distort, and modify the meaning of the elements they are supposed to carry' (2005:39). He argues that viewed through the lens of Actor-Network Theory (ANT), intermediaries would be rare and mediators common. Applying the notion of mediators to objects and devices associated with student digital engagement allows us to see them as active agents which influence and contribute to meaning-making, as opposed to neutral tools. (See Gourlay (2015) for a fuller discussion of this point in relation to academic writing). John Law makes this point in relation to textual practices:

> Almost all of our interactions with other people are mediated through objects of one kind or another. For instance, I speak to you through a text, even though we will probably never meet. And to do that, I am tapping away at a computer keyboard. At any rate, our communication with one another is mediated by a network of objects – the computer, the paper, the printing press. And it is also mediated by networks of objects-and-people, such as the postal system. The argument is that these various networks participate in the social. They shape it. In some measure they help to overcome your reluctance to read my text. And (most crucially) they are necessary to the social relationship between author and reader.
>
> *(Law 1992:380)*

Tara Fenwick and colleagues have explored the potential of sociomaterial perspectives for research in education more broadly, and propose the *assemblage* as a construct with which to understand how knowledge emerges through interaction with the nonhuman:

> Humans, and what they take to be their learning and social process, do not float, distinct, in container-like contexts of education, such a classrooms or community sites, that can be conceptualised and dismissed as simply a wash of material stuff and spaces. The things that assemble these contexts, and incidentally the actions and bodies including human ones that are part of these assemblages, are continuously acting upon each other to bring forth and distribute, as well as to obscure and deny, knowledge.
>
> *(Fenwick, Edwards and Sawchuk 2011:vii)*

As Bennett (2010) points out:

> A lot happens to the concept of agency once nonhuman things are figured less as social constructions and more as actors, and once humans themselves are assessed not as automatons but as vital materialities.
>
> *(Bennett 2010:21)*

The idea of the assemblage provides a rich way of understanding students' sociomaterial practices, and also helps to address the concerns raised in Chapters 4 and 5 about the focus for the analysis in this work. Viewing the assemblage, rather than the individual, as the unit of analysis helps to avoid romanticising and abstracting the free-floating student, showing instead how successful practice emerges through the interactions of agentive, situated people and things. It is only at the level of the assemblage that students' orientations, as described in Chapter 6, emerge. In the sections that follow, the relationships between these assemblages and students' study practices will be explored further.

Assemblages

In assemblages, 'each member and proto-member of the assemblage has a certain vital force, but there is also an effectivity proper to the grouping as such: an agency of the assemblage' (Bennett 2010:24). In the study, we found multiple examples of what could be termed *assemblages*, involving nonhuman actors in the form of digital devices and artefacts related to writing, such as paper, pens, Post-it notes and so on. The students were seen 'entangled' in various ways with print and digital devices and artefacts throughout the digital writing process.

The images in Figures 7.1–7.4 were produced by the students, and show assemblages of digital and print artefacts at the university, and also in the domestic environment. Other images and videos from the study depicted assemblages in public places and on transport (discussed more fully in Chapter 8).

FIGURE 7.1   Devices, from Yuki Interview 2

Decentring the Human

The student interview data revealed the interconnectedness of the various elements of the assemblages, in particular their perceptions of their entanglements with technologies both positive and problematic, as discussed in Gourlay and Oliver (2015):

> My third half of my brain is Google Scholar.
>
> *(Frederick Interview 2)*

Frederick jokes about Google Scholar being part of his brain, but in doing so he introduces a serious point about his knowledge and meaning-making practices not only residing in his own cognition, but also relying on interaction and entanglement with the internet. This seems to support our critique of mainstream notions of student engagement, which place the human centre stage as 'knower', relegating the internet and other texts as 'resources' to be accessed. Frederick's flippant comment suggests a different form of knowing and a different relationship to texts, one in which the human 'contracts out' the responsibility to store and organise information. This is arguably nothing new, and reflects one of the key functions of texts as repositories which endure and transcend time and space – however, with the advent of the internet this potential has increased exponentially.

> It's not necessarily the working with, sort of, the traditional practices, but much more about the, you know, our physical bodies in space, rather than . . . And thinking about online environments as being . . . the iPhone,

or whatever it is, connected to a projector, or working then with the iPad, and connecting, so you've got this kind of circuit within a physical space.

(Django Interview 1)

Django discusses her entanglements with technologies in her work around digital media and education, and in doing so makes specific reference to embodiment and space, referring to the assemblage as a 'circuit within a physical space'. This comment seems to exemplify the notion of the human/nonhuman assemblage.

As the discussion of students' orientations in Chapter 6 illustrated, students did not always feel in control of their technology. Sometimes, they struggled with it or ended up having to find workarounds because the technology would not do what they wanted. This sense of technology's agency is important analytically, as it helps to decentre humans in the analysis.

I think they (the technologies) control me as well, because I can't really do anything without them.

(Faith Interview 1)

FIGURE 7.2 iPad and papers, from Django Interview 2

FIGURE 7.3   Papers, books and hands, from Frederick Interview 2

Faith's comment reflects her feeling of being controlled by technologies, as she feels she cannot go about her engagement as a student teacher on placement without them. As she described in her example in Chapter 6, this was particularly true for lesson preparation, where she needs access to a networked computer and printer. Without the help of these technologies, she felt unable to operate successfully as a classroom teacher.

> So, I joined Twitter, and I didn't, I've just been listening to other people, I haven't been tweeting. But look, it's quite interesting: how does it know I'm friends with [name] and I like Katie Perry, may I ask? Like it already knew a lot about me, even when I joined. [. . .] I think it's quite in league with Facebook, I don't know, but I think a lot of these sites are like, integrated with each other now. They're quite, they're working together ways that you really don't know when you first enrol.
>
> *(Sally Interview 4)*

Finally, Sally's comment suggests a more troubled relationship with technologies, described in Chapter 6 as a 'combative' orientation. Here, she suggests she feels a sense of surveillance and invasion of her privacy. Elsewhere in the data, she refers to her phone as 'the spy in my pocket', and expressed concerns about her data being shared by commercial companies without her knowledge. There is little sense here of the technology as a neutral tool directed by the will of the user; these technologies are clearly not intermediators, in Latour's sense, but have a strong mediating influence on the practices they contribute to.

FIGURE 7.4   Bed and devices, from Nahid Interview 2

Materiality and Embodiment

In all of the comments above, the students express a relationship to the digital which seems to go beyond a straightforward tool and user interaction. Instead, digital texts and technologies are seen variously as part of cognition, joining the body to make a circuit, a controlling influence necessary for practice, or even an agent of surveillance.

This idea of humans forming part of circuits has arisen in discussions of educational technology, although with troubling overtones. Friesen (2004), for example, describes how the idea of humans as components in technical systems was of particular interest to the US military, who have been a major funder of educational technology research. Their metaphor of 'learning as a weapon system' drew on work in cybernetics, and repositioned learners as nodes in a system whose performance would need to be refined and improved. Although ANT can explain the emergence of this lack of human agency under specific conditions, this is not the sense in which we apply the idea here. Again, avoiding simplistic binaries (either having or not having agency), the focus of the analysis here is on the different kinds and degrees of agency that emerged from specific assemblages. Sally, for example, remains strongly agentive in the way she battled with technologies; and even in Faith's example with the printer, Faith was able to walk away from a situation where she felt technologies 'control me' and create an alternative that worked better for her instead.

However, this controlling perspective is only one among many ways of understanding embodied relationships with technology. Farr, Price and Jewitt (2012) describe a rich diversity of perspectives on embodiment, many tracing back to the Heidegger's exploration of the relationship between mind, body and knowledge. While psychological, sociological and engineering-based perspectives on this may differ, these all draw attention to the rich range of ways in which meaning is shaped by specific ways of being in the world.

The student research participants frequently described and represented practices in which a complex enmeshing of analogue and digital media was apparent. Texts were never purely digital for long, but instead moved between digital and analogue (print) formats as they were read, interacted with and also as they were produced. Students might encounter a text online, choose to print it, mark it up using highlighter pens or make handwritten notes on it, then they may convert the text back into typed notes, and so on. In TEL circles, the conventional explanation for adherence to analogue technologies, in place of new digital alternatives, has been that either the individual lacks the skills, or that they are resistant as a result of an aversion to the uptake of digital technologies. However, in the case of the students in the study, neither of these explanations seems to ring true – they were confident users of digital technologies, but their accounts of their practices showed that these were frequently combined with the analogue through preference. The students expressed a liking for the material qualities of pens, paper and books in particular – this did not seem to be related to functionality, but more to a desire to use these forms of embodied inscription practice, in addition to the (also embodied) engagement with the digital. Pen and paper technologies were mentioned by several students, suggesting a desire to handle and interact with the physical text through material artefacts by note making using marker pens, as when Frederick joked:

> When I read, it has to be a physical paper, and when I read I have my marker pen. So for me, a Kindle or something like that will not be an option for quite a long time, because I can't marker pen, or I could do it once but then it would be broken.
>
> *(Frederick Interview 1)*

For Louise, handwriting is preferred as it allows her to write in a different kind of way which does not allow for easy deletion of elements of her draft text:

> If I'm sitting at a computer typing, I find that really sort of blocks my thoughts because there's too much temptation to kind of delete and keep on changing. Whereas if you write by hand, you know, it just sort of flows more, I think. I mean, I guess like a lot of authors, I find it easier to write by hand than on a computer.
>
> *(Louise Interview 1)*

These comments suggest relationships with print literacy artefacts and practices which are not merely functional, in an efficiency-driven approach to tool use. Instead, there appears to be an element of preference which is more to do with the students' sense of affinity with the artefacts. Paying attention to these affective moments is important in moving beyond questions about whether or not a technology has been effective, or has been efficient, to consider other kinds of relationships that people develop with technologies, and through this to provide a much richer account of what motivates people to form assemblages with (or to avoid) technologies (Knox 2017). As Mulcahy (2012) has noted, such affective responses generate change: evoking distaste, excitement or care draws in or pushes away forms of engagement, producing pedagogic relationships that can change those involved.

This was also seen in some of the comments they made regarding their digital devices:

> And then I had a boyfriend at the time, and he had one of the little Apple Macs as well, so I got quite into using the whole kind of cute little thing. So, by the end of my college years I was quite in with the whole old-style Apple Mac.
>
> *(Sally Interview 1)*

> Actually, when I, yes, except for the sleep, I'm sleeping, I usually always touching my laptop.
>
> *(Yuki Interview 1)*

> I had to travel places far from my home or from the university, specially outside the capital in other parts of the country . . . I would still have my laptop with me so I could work on that. And later on, it was a constant company for me.
>
> *(Nahid Interview 1)*

These three comments seem to indicate a sense of affection or intimacy with the device, which again goes beyond functionality. These technologies are not simply efficient, they are also important: there is affection, care, and also a sense of being cared for. Instead of simply being a useful tool, with Yuki and Nahid we get a sense of the device as a 'companion' in private or solitary moments; in Yuki's case, she refers to constantly touching her laptop. Juan's representation of the production of an essay (see Figure 7.5), also discussed in detail in Gourlay (2015), is a striking example of this interweaving of the digital and the analogue:

Juan describes how he combines both the digital and the analogue in his scholarship practices:

> My favourite way of studying something is sitting down with a book and . . . a pen and some yellow paper and taking notes . . . And then I will use the technological side as well, because . . . Yes, I like combining the two, but I also like to be . . . the demarcation lines between them, you know, if I, if I have a reading to do then I can, then I almost, I invariably print it off and highlight and go through it and that kind of thing, then that's done, then I've got the notes, so then it's just the notes I've got.
>
> *(Juan Interview 1)*

Producing Academic texts (2)

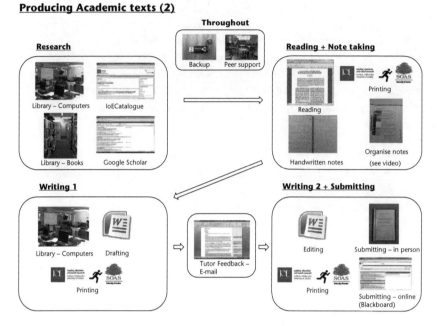

FIGURE 7.5 Juan's diagram

All of this is far removed from the idealistic, almost sterile discussions that take place about bodies in the TEL literature. This complexity tends to be ignored, or at least underestimated. The emphasis for several decades has been on 'de-materialising' the campus, with authors proposing that Google threatens 'the monopoly (or at least hegemony)' of lecturers and university libraries (Barber *et al.* 2013:16), or the popular press proposing that MOOCs will overthrow the 'brick and mortar' campus (e.g. Friedman 2013).

As Land has observed, such dreams are naïve:

> Even in cyberspace environments, as Stone (1991:117) has famously remarked, there is always 'a body attached'. Cyberspace could well be a non-space, but the subjects who inhabit it always remain embodied.
>
> *(Land 2005:154)*

In the social sciences, there has been renewed interest in bodily matters and embodied relations, including the body's materiality and boundaries. Jewitt, Price and Xambo Sedo (2017) develop these ideas to offer a view of the 'digital body', which questions what kinds of bodies are being constructed through the digital. From this, they develop the idea of the digital–physical trajectories of the body, exploring the movements of bodies across and between the digital and the physical.

This move permits, for example, the exploration of how people relate digital resources to physical spaces; or how they create new digital resources as they move to different physical spaces (Price, Jewitt and Sakr 2016).

From the interviews in this project, there is a wealth of evidence of intersections between study and other embodied activities, such as eating and sleeping, over a range of locations. Typically, mention of these intersections arose as part of the discussion of how studying fitted in around other activities, or how existing spaces were adapted so that they could also be used for studying. Yuki's discussion of the image of her iPad on the bath (see Chapter 6) was one example of this, as were comments like Polly's:

> The kitchen area has actually become quite nice and cosy to work in. Because of the table and because of the lighting it's quite nice to work there, so we can have a laptop there and we do that.
>
> *(Polly Interview 2)*

Given that study could require a sustained period of work, participants also described how important it was to them to make sure their working environment was comfortable.

> If I do want to read and have access to the computer, I'll do that in my room, and then I'll just have my desk opposite me with my screen, and I'll, sort of, sit sideways with my legs on the bed, stretched out, and my desk chair is pretty much like yours, so it reclines and it's very nice and comfortable.
>
> *(Frederick Interview 1)*

Nahid went further, linking changes in reading preferences to his sense of changes in his body.

> I've just bought a Kindle to read, and apart from that I also have a printer and I print out a lot. Because it's . . . maybe I'm getting old, or my eyes are getting old, something like that, but I can't read as much as I used to on the screen. I used to read a lot on the screen when I was in my graduation year or doing my past Master's, but now I don't feel that comfortable.
>
> *(Nahid Interview 1)*

This grounding in the material and embodied further undermines the notion of 'digital dualism' outlined in Chapter 3. Rather than a simplistic binary of either being embodied or liberated, it allows a more nuanced account to be developed of the different kinds of risks and constraints that arise in specific educational situations. Being online, Land argues, does not bring with it complete freedom – but neither does it degenerate into some kind of superficial experience, where digital mediation means that there is no risk, consequence or affect that might make the experience motivating and meaningful. Instead, it offers new ways to manage relationships and risks, leading Land to propose a relational approach to embodiment, mirroring the position taken here about the emergence of learners' qualities from the assemblages that are created.

> We can see how new technologies and artefacts (which would include language itself) have always reconstituted the embodiment of learners. We can see how the development of written culture created, for example, dyslexic learners, or the way that online environments created the 'lurkers'.
>
> *(Land 2005:161)*

It is not just learners, though, that are produced through the creation of these assemblages – knowledge is also produced, or obscured (Fenwick, Edwards and Sawchuk 2011). Dreyfus (2008) – one of the authors against whom Land (2005) reacts – argues against the possibility of meaningful learning taking place online. Although Dreyfus is concerned about the value of 'disembodied' learning experiences, his concerns are more to do with the ideas of *mediators* and *intermediaries* introduced earlier in this chapter. For him, being 'disembodied' is not about 'sloughing off our situated bodies' (50), but is instead about whether 'the mediated information concerning distant objects and people transmitted to us over the Internet as telepresence would be as present as anything could get' (54). The risk, he suggests, is that the mediation of the internet could result in impoverished, unsatisfactory experiences. A very different perspective on this issue, however, is offered by Ihde (2005). Ihde argues that the use of mediating technology should not be understood as a problem for learning, but as a necessary condition for it – this is not evidence of some revolution or singularity, but something ongoing and full of continuities and historical precedents. (This argument mirrors the position taken in Chapter 2.) Technologies, Ihde argues, have always been developed in order to make new kinds of presence and engagement possible. As such, they provide the material foundations for new forms of enquiry to be possible, whether in the form of familiar technologies (e.g. microscopes in biology), new technologies (e.g. particle accelerators in physics) or taken-for-granted technologies (e.g. writing in areas such as philosophy).

Examples of this kind of mediation of knowledge production can be seen in the accounts of participants. Frederick, for example, described how his work on datasets was shaped by the software that was available to support his multi-level modelling, and the expertise that others had built up in using it to support conceptual claims.

> I spent a few days trying to explore what kind of models exist that account for measurement error in variables. And I found a few things, but I found that without some expert giving me a little bit of an introduction on what the concepts are, or especially looking then at Stata, which of these models can Stata actually do, I couldn't carry on.
>
> *(Frederick Interview 4)*

Django, similarly, talked about taking photographs and editing video in order to create materials for teaching pupils in a London gallery, and how 'a lot of the work was quite graphics based' (Django Interview 2). Juan also described the way he developed a specific questionnaire, in order to create data for his dissertation. This might be a less obvious technology than cameras or software packages, but as Bowker and Star (1999) describe, classification schemes can act as a technology that shapes peoples' worlds through the way they are or are not allowed to describe their lives. Echoing Land's point above about language itself being a technology that can reconstitute learners, Juan described how the implementation of a survey for teachers in an Arabic-speaking country had required flights and translators, and had positioned him as an outsider for part of his own project.

> Originally, I planned to do it from a distance, [. . .] I thought I could just send some questionnaires and they would help and distribute it and send it back. [. . .] Luckily, there are easyJet flights, so I could go there and do that. [. . .] And then the more I sort of looked at it, I realised it would be . . . it would take somebody quite a long time to translate it. [. . .] I tried to get it done here, and in the end, I had to get it done in Jordan, and I had to get it done by . . . I had to pay to get it done, because I thought it was such a long thing, I thought I'll pay to get it done and then have somebody check it. And that was wrong, because I know they translated it literally, obviously, and I needed it to be a bit more, sort of, nuanced. So yes, in the end it was a bit of a nightmare and I only got it done sort of the day before I was supposed to be doing it.
>
> *(Juan Interview 4)*

Excerpts such as these show that, as with the orientations described in Chapter 5, the use of technologies sometimes involved struggle and workarounds. The use of technology to support claims about knowledge involved both struggles with the thing itself (as in Frederick's attempts to learn how to use Stata) as well as struggles in bringing the technology to bear on the world (as with Juan's attempts to distribute a survey to participants in another country).

Conclusions

This chapter opened with the idea of the nonhuman actor, and the proposal that objects and devices should not just be seen as inert tools that people use, but as agentive actors in their own right, contributing to the creation of assemblages, and transforming the other components of the networks that they come into contact with. Throughout the chapter, we have explored how technologies have acted as *mediators* rather than *intermediaries*, translating, distorting and moderating meaning rather than simply carrying it in some transparent way.

This undermines the idea that students can be understood simply as users of tools. Instead, students are redefined by the tools that they use. Frederick, with and without 'contracting out' expertise to Google Scholar, with and without the analytical power of Stata, is a different kind of student, able to make very different kinds of claims to knowledge. These technologies do not just provide access to information for him, but instead draw attention to certain pieces of knowledge – and, as Fenwick, Edwards and Sawchuk (2011) pointed out – obscuring others. Juan's expertise in designing surveys was obscured by his inability to speak Arabic; Louise's ability to write fluently was interrupted by the ease of constant editing and deleting.

Throughout these processes, students are living with technology. They touch it, carry it and form attachments to it – or find that it makes them uncomfortable, resent it and leave it behind. They take their technologies into private, intimate spaces – the bed, the bath – in order to create the environments that they need in order to study. These are not simply 'found' contexts, spaces for them to occupy or to float through unencumbered by material concerns. These places are full of things that push back, reshaping students at the same time that they are being reshaped. The next chapter will develop these ideas further, looking beyond the technologies that live alongside students to the environments that they all inhabit, raising questions about the assumed neutral status of space and time in practices and student engagement, arguing instead for a perspective which sees these as agentive and co-constitutive, in a reflexive relationship with practices and subjectivities, online and offline.

References

Barber, M., Donnelly, K., Rizvi, S. and Summers, L. 2013. *An Avalanche Is Coming*. London: Institute for Public Policy Research. www.ippr.org/publication/55/10432/an-avalanche-iscoming-higher-education-and-the-revolution-ahead [Accessed 10 Aug 2017].
Bennett, J. 2010. *Vibrant Matter: A Political Ecology of Things*. London: Duke University Press.
Bowker, G. and Star, S. 1999. *Sorting Things Out: Classification and its Consequences*. Cambridge, MA: MIT Press.
Clarke, J. 2002. A new kind of symmetry? Actor-network theories and the new literacy studies. *Studies in the Education of Adults* 34(2), 107–122.
Dreyfus, H. (2008). *On the Internet*. London: Routledge.
Farr, W., Price, S. and Jewitt, C. 2012. An introduction to embodiment and digital technology research: interdisciplinary themes and perspectives. *National Centre for Research Methods Working Paper* 02/12. London: Institute of Education.
Fenwick, T., Edwards, R. and Sawchuk, P. 2011. *Emerging Approaches to Educational Research: Tracing the Sociomaterial*. London: Routledge.
Friedman, T. 2013. Revolution hits the universities. *The New York Times*, 26th Jan.
Friesen, N. 2004. Three objections to learning objects and e-learning standards. In R. McGreal (Ed.), *Online Education Using Learning Objects*. London: RoutledgeFalmer, 59–70.
Goodfellow, R. and Lea, M. 2007. *Challenging E-learning in the University: A Literacies Perspective*. London: Routledge.
Goodfellow, R. and Lea, M. 2013. *Literacy in the Digital University: Critical Perspectives on Learning, Scholarship and Technology*. London: Routledge.

Gourlay, L. 2015. Posthuman texts: nonhuman actors, mediators and the digital university. *Social Semiotics* 25(4), 484–500.

Gourlay, L. and Oliver, M. 2015. It's not all about the learner. A sociomaterial reframing of students' digital literacy practices. In T. Ryberg, S. Bayne, C. Sinclair and M. de Laat (Eds.), *Research, Boundaries, and Policy in Networked Learning*. London: Routledge, 77–92. https://link.springer.com/chapter/10.1007%2F978-3-319-31130-2_5 [Accessed 10 Aug 2017].

Gourlay, L., Hamilton, M. and Lea, M. 2013. Textual practices in the new media landscape: messing with digital literacies. *Research in Learning Technologies* 21(1), 1–13.

Hamilton, M. 2011. Unruly practices: what a sociology of translations can offer to educational policy analysis. In T. Fenwick and R. Edwards (Eds.), *Journal of Educational Philosophy and Theory* Special Issue on Actor-Network Theory 43(1), 55–75.

Ihde, D. 2005. More material hermeneutics. *Yearbook of the Institute for Advanced Studies on Science, Technology and Society*. Munich, Germany: Profil Verlag, 341–350.

Jewitt, C., Price, S. and Xambo Sedo, A. 2017. Conceptualising and researching the body in digital contexts: towards new methodological conversations across the arts and social sciences. *Qualitative Research* 17(1), 37–53.

Knox, H. 2017. Affective Infrastructures and the Political Imagination. *Public Culture* 29(2), 363–384.

Land, R. 2005. Embodiment and risk in cyberspace education. In R. Land and S. Bayne (Eds.), *Education in Cyberspace*. London: Routledge, 149–164.

Lankshear, C. and Knobel, M. 2008. *Digital Literacies: Concepts, Policies and Practices*. Oxford: Peter Lang.

Latour, B. 2005. *Reassembling the Social: An Introduction to Actor-Network-Theory*. Oxford: Oxford University Press.

Law, J. 1992. Notes on the theory of the actor-network: ordering, strategy, and heterogeneity. *Systemic Practice and Action Research* 5(4), 379–393.

Lea, M. 2007. Emerging literacies in online learning. *Journal of Applied Linguistics* 4(1), 79–100.

Lea, M. and Jones, S. 2011. Digital literacies in higher education: exploring textual and technological practice. *Studies in Higher Education* 36(4), 377–393.

Leander, K. and Lovvorn, J. 2006. Literacy networks: following the circulation of texts, bodies and objects in the schooling and online gaming of one youth. *Cognition and Instruction* 24(3), 291–340.

Mulcahy, D. 2012. Affective assemblages: body matters in the pedagogic practices of contemporary school classrooms. *Pedagogy, Culture & Society* 20(1), 9–27.

Price, S., Jewitt, C. and Sakr, M. 2016. Embodied experiences of place: a study of history learning with mobile technologies. *Journal of Computer Assisted Learning* 32(4), 345–359.

Williams, B. 2009. *Shimmering literacies: Popular culture & reading & writing online*. Oxford: Peter Lang.

8
BEYOND CONTEXT

In the previous chapters we have looked at and questioned categories placed on students. In doing so, we have sought to move away from abstract conceptions of students and student engagement in terms of typologies, skills or attributes, and towards a focus on practices. We have also argued that the central role of meaning-making and also the digital in student engagement have been overlooked in mainstream accounts of the Higher Education curriculum. We have proposed, drawing on New Literacy Studies, that these practices – and therefore student engagement – are always socially situated, as opposed to residing primarily in the minds of individuals; and in the last chapter we argued that student engagement is also sociomaterially situated, drawing on sociomaterial perspectives and ANT. In this regard, we have attempted to provide a more nuanced and situated understanding of student digital engagement as it actually unfolds in the day-to-day. Throughout this account there is a focus on moving away from the notion of the individual floating in neutral 'contexts' – instead, the social, textual, nonhuman and material are in constant interaction with the student, co-constituting practices, texts and the students themselves.

This chapter aims to challenge the notion of context further, by turning our attention to the status and role of space and time. These are – in common-sense terms and in the mainstream of educational literature – regarded as 'background' to practice, the settings or 'boxes' in which practice takes place. This view is understandable – our day-to-day perception is arguably that space and time are forms of neutral 'openings' in which we conduct our lives or our educational engagement. However, an alternative view would see these as more active agents in engagement – this view will be explored below.

'Learning Spaces'

The importance of space in Higher Education has been increasingly recognised recently (e.g. JISC 2006, Temple 2007, Finkelstein *et al.* 2014, UCISA 2016), in contrast with the school sector where there has been a more long-standing recognition of the importance of the issue (Clark 2002). The influence of layout, interior design and furniture on student engagement in classrooms, and also in public areas, such as libraries and study areas, has come to be recognised across the sector, and is frequently discussed in terms of 'learning spaces'. This section will examine how this concept has been deployed, and the values and beliefs surrounding student engagement (both online and offline) which underpin how the contemporary sector approaches space.

In a literature review of the area, Temple (2007) highlights several documents which had recently emerged. The UK Joint Information Services Committee document entitled 'Designing Spaces for Effective Learning: A Guide to 21st Century Learning Design' (JISC 2006), for example, was aimed at senior managers and decision-makers in universities, in order to support them to '. . . keep abreast of new thinking about the design of technology-rich spaces' (JISC 2006:2). We will spend some time looking at this document in detail as a representation of how space and the digital was understood in relation to student engagement.

It states that '. . . the design of our learning spaces should become a physical representation of the institution's vision and strategy for learning' (JISC 2006:2) – here the design is explicitly connected with beliefs surrounding what is considered to be desirable student engagement. At the beginning, it sets out that the design should exhibit the following features:

- Flexible – to accommodate both current and evolving pedagogies
- Future-proofed – to enable space to be re-allocated and reconfigured
- Bold – to look beyond tried and tested technologies and pedagogies
- Creative – to energise and inspire learners and tutors
- Supportive – to develop the potential of all learners
- Enterprising – to make each space capable of supporting different purposes.

(JISC 2006:2)

This is followed by the statement that:

A learning space should be able to motivate learners and promote learning as an activity, support collaboration as well as formal practice, provide a personalised and inclusive environment, and be flexible in the face of changing needs. The part technology plays in achieving these aims is the focus of this guide.

(JISC 2006:2)

The predominance of the word 'learning' is noteworthy throughout the document, particularly the emphasis in the above quote on 'learning as an activity'. The guide goes on to focus on informal open-plan 'learning areas' and places a strong emphasis on inculcating student collaboration in these areas. It begins by defining these areas as for student use outside of timetabled classes, although it also refers to the need for '. . . large open centres where both learning and teaching take place' (JISC 2006:5). It appears that learning is being used here to refer to study-related practices outside of timetabled classes; it also appears to be seen as non-concurrent with 'teaching'. An example is given of a networked learning café with PCs, designed to support group work and problem-based learning. In the description of the learning café, it states that it is a place '. . . where conversation and social interaction are an essential part of learning' (JISC 2006:5). It is worth drawing attention here to how verbal interaction is explicitly portrayed not just as desirable for certain types of group activities, but as an *essential* prerequisite for learning itself.

The next section is entitled 'Transforming Learning Experiences', and focuses on the technological infrastructure of the institution. It lists a range of technologies, but is mostly composed of two page-sized illustrations (JISC 2006:6–7). These show large open-plan areas with most of the figures in groups around tables, screens and whiteboards. There are no classrooms or lecture theatres shown, although teaching appears to be taking place in one small part of the first illustration in an open-plan area divided by a screen. There is no library and only one bookcase is depicted, again in an open-plan area next to a table being used for group work. A solitary figure from around 60 people in the illustrations appears be taking a book from a shelf; apart from that individual there do not seem to be any students reading or writing using non-digital media, with very few shown working alone at screens. Instead, nearly all the figures in the illustrations are shown to be interacting in open-plan areas of various types, in front of screens. The next part of the guide focuses on the features of university entrances and reception areas, stating that:

> Entering a college or university building should create a sense of excitement about learning. The entrance is the first point of contact between the institution and its clients and will establish the prevailing culture for visitors. Its next priority is to offer clear, accessible information about the institution and what can be achieved there. An entrance area will also need to provide a welcoming, secure environment, establishing the capability of the institution to cater for its learners – after all, it has to compete for learners' time and attention with the shopping mall, the leisure centre, and facilities and technologies within the home.
>
> *(JISC 2006:8)*

The university is explicitly framed here as an institution which must 'compete for learners' time and attention' against shopping malls or leisure centres, with the stated aim that the university entrance is to appear worthy of students' time and attention, in the face of apparently competing outlets and providers of entertainment. This is a strikingly explicit expression of Higher Education as a provider of a commodity, positioning the students explicitly as customers who must be attracted and satisfied.

The guide goes on to describe an idealised reception area, where digital technologies are used in a range of ways to provide information for students, stating that in this ideal space:

> ... a proactive service-delivery culture ensures that reception staff respond helpfully to the needs of visitors, assisted by a range of information outlets. The ambience is calm and authoritative. Brightly-lit, spacious and architecturally impressive, the entrance area inspires interest and respect.
>
> *(JISC 2006:8)*

A range of services is provided in this imagined reception area, and it is suggested that music or the local radio station should be played, '. . . providing travel information and a calming effect on those passing through' (*ibid.*).

The students, it seems, are simultaneously positioned by these statements in several ways. They are described as potential customers in a way which echoes the 'student experience' discourse critiqued in Chapter 1, which in itself seems odd as – apart from on open days – once enrolled at the university, the students have already made their choice. However, it appears that the university should continue to court them on an ongoing basis as customers who may become distracted by the attractions of shopping, leisure or entertainment. The students are also apparently positioned rather like visitors to a large company which provides some sort of personalised service – their 'needs' are assessed individually on arrival via a 'proactive service-delivery culture'.

However, the statement also includes the notion that the ambience should also be 'authoritative', and should 'inspire respect'. This complicates the intended semiotics of the entrance area – which it appears should also have the ambience of an 'authoritative' institution. This seems to contradict the preceding points, which clearly position the student as a consumer whose needs must be satisfied in a competitive landscape of rival commercial and entertainment attractions. The addition of music to provide a 'calming atmosphere' is reminiscent of a waiting room, and suggests that the students are potentially nervous clients – the job of the university is apparently to soothe them on arrival. It is also reminiscent of the social anthropologist Marc Augé's 'non-place' – a smooth transit space, as opposed to the 'place', which can be defined as relational, historical and concerned with identity. He explores the tensions between these two extremes:

> Place and non-place are rather like opposing polarities: the first is never completely erased, the second never totally completed; they are like palimpsests on which the scrambled game of identity and relations is ceaselessly rewritten.
>
> *(Augé 1995:79)*

As we have seen above, the students are portrayed as consumers or clients, but also as subject to the 'authority' of the university. In addition, the illustrations and statements argue (pictorially and in the written text) that interaction is not only desirable, but is a prerequisite to learning. At no point is the student portrayed as a member of a scholarly community, and engagement with academic expertise, teaching, knowledge and scholarship is entirely absent from the description. This example serves as an illustration of the fundamentally confused discourses surrounding students in the contemporary sector, the multiple nature of the various positionalities imposed on them, and the incoherent and over-simplistic discourses surrounding their engagement, which we have been exploring throughout this book.

The statement in this guide on 'teaching spaces' is as follows:

> General teaching spaces have been dominated in the last century by one type of design: tutor-focused, one-way facing and presentational, with seating arranged in either a U-shape or in straight rows. Technologies have subsequently been added – interactive or conventional white boards mounted on the wall behind the main speaker, ceiling-mounted projectors with cabling to a laptop, a wireless network or wired computers – but these have rarely altered the dynamics of the design.
>
> *(JISC 2006:10)*

Here, the lecture theatre or classroom is characterised as 'tutor-focused'. The document goes on to make the statement that '. . . the prevailing pedagogic approach has swung towards active and collaborative learning' (*ibid.*), with the implication being that lecture theatres and classrooms are no longer fit for purpose. The accompanying illustration shows what appear to be three lecturers teaching groups of around five students each, all in the same room with a screen dividing one of the groups from the other two – this in itself seems an unlikely arrangement for teaching, as it would involve a great deal of noise. It is not clear how large classes are to be taught in this model. The section on 'collaboration' states:

> Learners have been shown to benefit academically from social interaction with their peers. Open-plan informal learning areas provide individualised learning environments which also support collaborative activities, and they can often be created from previously underutilised spaces. An example is the internet café. In many institutions, entrance spaces now include open-access IT areas with refreshments and informal seating. Utilisation data have proved the worth of such areas – their value lies in the way they encourage learning through dialogue, problem solving and information sharing in the most supportive of contexts.
>
> *(JISC 2006:4)*

The statement above emphasises interactivity and dialogue. Teaching is described as follows:

> The design of most general teaching spaces will usually need to support both tutor-led and learner-led activities. These will include presentations, discussion, collaborative project work, and information retrieval and sharing.
>
> *(JISC 2006:10–11)*

Although these are all legitimate and useful activities, the guide seems to omit some of the fundamental elements of Higher Education, and restricts it to collaborative activity and 'information retrieval' only, eliding criticality, advanced scholarship and the generation of new knowledge in a way somewhat reminiscent of 'connectivism', as discussed in Chapter 2. Lectures are (once again) implied to be retrograde; teaching and expertise are portrayed as 'tutor-centred' and seem to be largely absent or downplayed in the model. Private study, silence, reading or writing is not mentioned. Legitimate student engagement is apparently restricted to entirely collaborative discursive practices and based in small groups in open-plan settings.

Digital technologies are deployed in the model in a way which apparently underscores the 'student-as-consumer' model – it is noteworthy that the role of technologies is described in most detail in the section on the entrance and reception area. The ways in which students might engage with the digital in their study practices, and how these might qualitatively influence their scholarship, are not explored. Instead, despite digital technologies being the stated focus of the guide, the way they are presented remains at a somewhat abstracted level, with only lists of devices and platforms provided. *How* students might actually engage in space, and how they might make choices and interact with technology is not explored, and research into student engagement is not referred to, with both spatial design and digital infrastructure being assumed to be in a one-way deterministic relationship with practices.

Instead, the focus of the guide seems to point elsewhere – it is suffused with expressions of the two conflicting ideologies discussed in the introduction – 'the student experience', which positions the student as a customer, and an unnuanced notion of 'student engagement', which claims to support 'student-centred learning' and promote pedagogic innovation and interactivity. However, in doing so, this underscores what can justifiably be described as an anti-intellectual agenda, and it also appears to 'throw the baby out with the bathwater' by disavowing some of the fundamentals of Higher Education and advanced scholarship.

More recently, *The UK Higher Education Learning Space Toolkit* (UCISA 2016) was produced by SCHOMS (Standing Conference for Heads of Media Services), AUDE (Association of University Directors of Estates) and UCISA (University and Colleges Information Systems Association). This is a longer, more nuanced and more detailed document aimed as professional service staff in charge of estates development. In the introduction, the need for both 'formal' and 'informal' spaces is acknowledged. The section on pedagogy states that:

> We need to design for a diversity of pedagogic approaches bearing in mind a strong prevailing tendency towards a socio-constructivist approach that emphasises participatory and collaborative activities wherever appropriate.
>
> *(UCISA 2016:8)*

It uses the term 'built pedagogy', which Monaghan (2002) used to describe 'architectural embodiments of educational philosophies'. This is used to reflect the belief that 'the way in which a space is designed shapes the learning that takes place in that space' (UCISA 2016:9).

There is a predominant emphasis on the encouragement of interaction, in particular verbal interaction which is evidenced by the tendency to create communal discussion areas, the move away from 'quiet' libraries, and the apparent desire to avoid 'closed' or private spaces in favour of open and observable areas. This indicates two underlying beliefs. As with the earlier document, the first is that face-to-face interaction is to be preferred over quiet or individual study. Although interaction is clearly important, it might be argued that these designs carry with them an implicit or even explicit disapproval of practices which do not accord with, or instantiate, this belief. Therefore, quiet study arguably begins to be seen as retrograde, despite the ongoing reliance on individual assessment across the sector. The second is the belief that the design of space is straightforwardly deterministic, and that it will lead students unproblematically to certain practices, or forms of engagement. This belief assumes a strong degree of agency on the part of space and the built environment, and perhaps underestimates the degree to which the students adapt and make space their own, according to their preferences and the demands of the task at hand.

Entangling with Space

In an apparently contradictory development, early commentary surrounding student engagement with the digital tended to characterise it as leading to a free-floating state, with the use of phrases, such as 'any time, any place' learning (e.g. Hiltz and Wellman 1997), as was discussed in Chapter 7 with reference to materiality and embodiment. The 'virtuality' of educational experiences was associated with a detachment (or 'freedom') from spatial and temporal settings (e.g. Hamilton and Zimmerman 2002). As discussed in Gourlay and Oliver (2016) and above, this can be attributed to what Land (2005) has called 'the incorporeal fallacy', in which bodies and material spaces are imagined to disappear via digital engagement. Space is seen as an impediment or restriction to be overcome in this discourse. Knox (2013) has pointed out the tendency in discussions of Open Educational Resources (OERs) to regard institutional spaces as constraining 'unfreedoms'. Throughout the literature on 'flexible learning', there is a persistent fantasy that digital technologies confer the potential to transcend not only embodiment and materiality, but space itself. The physical campus is denigrated as retrograde, limiting or even obsolete, as we saw in the 'brave new world' discourses critiqued in Chapter 2. It must be 'transformed' into a purely collaborative and interactive space, or alternatively, escaped from entirely. This is also reminiscent of the 'digital dualism' discussed in Chapter 2 – the digital and analogue are presented as an either/or binary, with the digital assumed to be superior in all respects.

This is not to say, however, that the prevalence of digital technologies in Higher Education has had no effect on practices, or does not provide more flexible options for students. Clearly, access to networked devices on campus and while on the move has led to profound changes to student engagement. However, as Land points out, the notion of incorporeality is indeed a fallacy – all engagement with devices is embodied, in the sense that the human body is always present and is in contact with the device, and all of it is materially situated – it happens in a particular place, which could be the library, the home, public transport and so on. The texts and images may be digital, but the practices are still particular, material and spatial – what Hayles (1996, 1999) calls 'embodied virtuality'.

There is also a concurrent tendency in educational thought (and social science more broadly) for space to be seen as a neutral context or backdrop to human intentionality and activity, a kind of empty box. However, this view has been challenged perhaps most prominently by the human geographer Doreen Massey, who urges us to see space as an active and co-constitutive agent in social process – both a product of relations and a contributor to practices:

> We recognise space as the product of interrelations; as constituted through interactions, from the immensity of the global to the intimately tiny. [. . .] We recognise space as always under construction. Precisely because space on this reading is a product of relations-between, relations which are necessarily embedded in material practices which have to be carried out, it is always in the process of being made. It is never finished; never closed. Perhaps we could imagine space as a simultaneity of stories-so-far.
>
> *(Massey 2005:9)*

This framing of space as part of or a product of interrelations, provides us with an alternative to viewing space as either a rigid and unmovable constraint which must be fully transcended through incorporeality or transformation, or a neutral and inert 'context' or backdrop. Instead, we can theorise space as a fluid, relational entity which can shape practice, but also in turn can be shaped by it. As Hannam *et al.* put it, there is a need for an approach which:

> . . . problematizes both 'sedentarist' approaches in the social science that treat place, stability and dwelling as a natural steady-state, and 'deterritorialized'

> approaches that posit a new 'grand narrative' of mobility, fluidity or liquidity
> as a pervasive condition of postmodernity or globalization.
>
> *(Hannam, Sheller and Urry 2006:5)*

In a paper written with the library ethnographer Donna Lanclos, we looked at student interaction with spaces in their engagement with independent study, and also in library use (Gourlay, Oliver and Lanclos 2015). In this study, we explored student relationships to the space in the material campus, and found them to be more interactive and emergent than suggested by the notion discussed above, which implied that space is predictably constitutive of student practice or engagement. Instead, the visual data created by the student in the form of diagrams and 'maps' depicted them in complex interplay with campus spaces, which they are seen to inhabit and adapt in idiosyncratic ways, often involving personalisation of space and a sensitivity to materiality, even in spaces intended for free-floating digital use, such as hot desks. Embodiment and the needs of the body were prominent in the interview data, with preferences in terms of hot drinks, comfort, quiet and a sense of belonging frequently mentioned.

In the JISC study, students were asked in the first interview to draw a diagram, picture or map to depict their everyday study practices and engagement with the digital. Nahid, an international Master's student, identified three main domains of engagement in terms of space: the physical campus (IOE), transport and home. His A4 drawing with notes is shown in Figures 8.1–3 in his three boxed sections.

The first box on his drawing shown in Figure 8.1 refers to his engagement in the university campus. He identifies the library, in particular the computers, where he notes that he goes to search the catalogue, work on assignments, search for online material and check emails. He also uses his laptop in the library to 'do usual things'. The second space he refers to is the lobby, where he uses his phone to text or try to log in to the Wi-Fi network.

The second box in Nahid's drawing refers to his home, shown in Figure 8.2. His laptop is depicted in the centre, with a wide range of forms of engagement noted against it. These include university-related activities, such as accessing Blackboard (the virtual learning environment used at that time in the institution), using the student portal, locating sources online, working on essays, researching and using university email. He also includes a range of leisure activities, such as listening to online radio, watching movies, online shopping and reading online newspapers. He also lists the social networking platforms Facebook, Yahoo Messenger and Skype.

Nahid's third and final box in Figure 8.3 refers to his engagement while on public transport. He shows his Kindle for reading books and his phone, which he uses for a range of purposes – reading old emails, listening to music, checking times of appointments or room numbers and making calls.

Students were also asked to represent their engagement using PowerPoint or another presentation platform. Yuki produced the image shown in Figure 8.4.

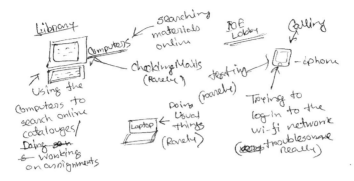

FIGURE 8.1 Nahid's map (detail 1)

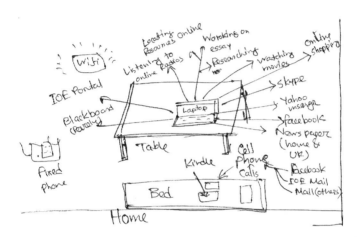

FIGURE 8.2 Nahid's map (detail 2)

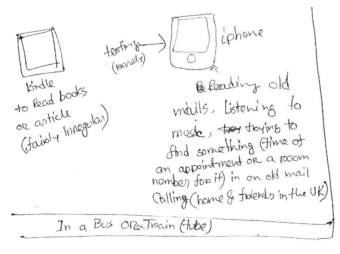

FIGURE 8.3 Nahid's map (detail 3)

FIGURE 8.4 PowerPoint slide, Yuki Interview 3

Yuki presented this collage of images which represents the range of locations where she engages with study practices, both digital and print based. She describes her mobile practice as follows:

> For me the most important thing is portability, because I use technologies, ICT, everywhere I go, anywhere I go. For example, of course I use some technologies, PCs and laptops and my iPad in the [institutional] building, and in the [institutional] building I use PC, I use them in PC room, in library, and for searching some data or journals. In the lecture room I record my, record the lectures and taking memos by that.
>
> *(Yuki Interview 1)*

In the case of both Nahid and Yuki, we see human/nonhuman assemblages emerging in transitory spaces, such as on transport, standing in hallways and in the park. They are mobile, but always situated in the particular. Here, in place of assumed incorporeality, the practices are tethered to the moving body across a range of spaces which are described in very particular material terms. These are assemblages of practice which are fluid, contingent and emergent – but at the same time, they are carefully curated, fragile and materially bounded. The various devices and platforms were combined to make 'moorings' (Hannam, Sheller and

Urry 2006, Urry 2007). The importance of specific spaces was emphasised by Juan in the study:

> I enjoy . . . the image of being, sort of, in a dusty, you know, sort of, wooden shelved, kind of, old library, where it's, sort of, cosy and warm, that's, you know, I like that and that's a part of the experience of studying that I enjoy.
>
> *(Juan Interview 1)*

He also remarks:

> Where I live it could be, you could be in a town sort of anywhere and you wouldn't really necessarily notice. Whereas you come in here and you come over the Waterloo Bridge and you see St Paul's and the Houses of Parliament, you know, you're in London, you're doing something again. You know, this is where people do important things and that, kind of, thing and it gives it a reality. [. . .] It focuses me a little bit on that.
>
> *(Juan Interview 3)*

These images and quotes from the students suggest a more complex and multi-faceted relationship with space than that which would be predicted either by a model viewing space as neutral context on one hand, or as straightforwardly deterministic on the other (as implied by the 'learning spaces' literature). Instead, the students appear to interact and negotiate with space, which is agentive and constitutive, without being rigidly deterministic. They seem markedly sensitive to location and mobilities in their practices, and their assemblages are ephemeral, contingent and somewhat fragile in terms of space, requiring careful attention in order to be able to emerge. Space and mobilities also seem to play a close role in what practices emerge and thrive, which devices are used and how they are used. However, it is worth noting that this does not reflect practical access and efficacy alone – preferences, emotions and a sense of curation and delineation of space clearly played a part in how the student chose to entangle with space. The next section will look at how time also played a role in these assemblages of practice.

Entangling with Time

As with space, there is a tendency in educational research and thought to assume time is also a neutral backcloth to activity, an empty container in which educational activity takes place. However, in philosophy and social theory, the nature and complexity of time has been explored and these assumptions have been questioned. Grosz considers its nature:

> Time is neither fully 'present', a thing in itself, nor is it a pure abstraction, a metaphysical assumption that can be ignored in everyday practice. It cannot be viewed directly, nor can it be eliminated from pragmatic consideration.

It is a kind of evanescence that appears only at those moments when we are jarred out of our immersion in its continuity, when something untimely disrupts our expectations.

(Grosz 2004:5)

The central role of time in relation to social and cultural practices has been explored by Elizabeth Adam in a series of influential publications (Adam 1995, 2004, 2006). Adam demonstrates the way that time, and how it is measured and perceived, plays an important constitutive role in how human life emerges. Lemke (2000) looks at networks of semiotic practice, proposing books as 'boundary objects' which can be used to co-ordinate across timescales:

The notebook, as a material object with semiotic affordances, as a thing that can also be a sign, materially links two events across time and space and so participates in a process on a much longer timescale than either the event of writing or the event of reading that particular note. And in this case so also does the student. At another juncture, the teacher reads aloud from the textbook, writes on the board, and asks a question that would not have been written or asked as it was without the influence of the textbook's words. Those words, the generic discourse pattern or discourse formation inscribed in the material object of the textbook, have an even longer (cultural) history than does the particular material book or the unique wording of its text. Not only the processes and activities that produced the textbook, but also the processes and activities that produced that standard discourse pattern about chemical reactions and circulated it long ago to the textbook's authors and editors, are now intersecting through the mediation of the book as a material-semiotic object with the much shorter-term events in the classroom episode.

(Lemke 2000:281)

Lemke is emphasising what he proposes is the agentive nature of these objects, which have the capacity to co-produce educational process in terms of its temporal nature. He also draws out the agentive nature of the book's contribution to the shorter temporal frame of the classroom encounter. This property of a semiotic object, such as a book (and texts in general), to link ideas and meaning-making across time is perhaps something we take for granted, and has therefore become 'invisible'.

Returning to the digital, Horning, Ahrens and Gerhard (1999) posed the question of how technologies might 'entime' social practice and engagement. They looked at new communications technologies of the period and, in an interview study, investigated different responses to them by individuals. They invoke the Heideggerian stance that:

... time is part of our physical involvement with the natural and technological world; our practical daily involvement with the material world is temporal to its core. Time is then more than a socially constructed category that allows us to move through the world in a coordinated and meaningful fashion. Instead human beings establish peculiar temporal relations with the world; they are locked into the material and technological words that they create.

(Horning, Ahrens and Gerhard 1999:294)

Horning *et al.* draw on Latour (2004) to explore the mediating role of artefacts in relation with time:

Practical life is a continual blend of routine and thought. New knowledge and new technologies permanently open up new strands of involvement with the world. Then the already learned skills and competences to enact and 'entime' the world become inappropriate and are confronted with the contingencies of new knowledge and recent technology.

(Horning, Ahrens and Gerhard 1999:297)

They pose a series of questions exploring the role of technologies in 'entiming' social action, whether 'time regimes' are built into technologies, also asking '. . . how do the temporalities of technology relate to the various temporalities embedded in different social practices?' (Horning, Ahrens and Gerhard 1999:24). Their analysis of the (then new) technologies of the PC, the video and the telephone answering machine shows what they classified as three patterns of engagement among the research participants. The *surfer* was found to use technologies to save time, with an emphasis on accelerated pace and time being viewed as a scarce resource. The *sceptic* was found to prefer face-to-face engagement and print technologies, and viewed time as an entity to be used meaningfully, rather than efficiently. The third figure identified in the study was the *gambler*, who they characterised as flexible and adaptable, seeking to generate time margins in new ways. In relation to this study, the interrelationship between the student practices and time was explored in Gourlay (2014). In that analysis, a series of relationships was also found between the students' entanglements with technologies and time. Unlike Horning *et al.*, categories were not attached to participant orientations, but instead several themes arose.

The first of these was *slowness* – several students commented that technologies caused their practices to slow down, or may even have caused them to abandon or change their plans, such as Juan's account of working with the library database:

So, they listed journals but they didn't list internal articles in the journals, so even if they were accessible online, you didn't know. That was . . . that was something that really slowed down the process and did, sort of, make you think well, I might as well go and sift through them by hand rather than do it by . . . so I think that was a big one.

(Juan Interview 1)

He also reports an occasion when he tried to use a piece of software, but gave up on the plan as it was taking too long to work out how to use it:

> I assume I will be able to do something, and then if it takes longer than five minutes, I then dismiss it as rubbish. So rather than give it the six or seven minutes that it requires just to figure out how to do it once well.
>
> *(Juan Interview 2)*

E-books were also rejected by another participant due to the slowness of the Wi-Fi network:

> I don't like, yes, I don't like e-books because sometimes I can't access because my, as I mentioned, Wi-Fi access in my room was very poor so sometimes suddenly it was disconnected so I cannot go to . . . move to the next page.
>
> *(Yuki Interview 2)*

These accounts of online engagement being cumbersome or slow because of the infrastructure appears to contradict the 'brave new world' fantasies of hyper-efficiency critiqued earlier in the book. Instead, the student accounts reveal engagement which is not smooth and frictionless. The students report decision-making around engagement with technology which centres on whether it will in fact be a worthwhile or useful investment of time.

The second theme that arose from the data centred on *overload*, which the students also related to slowness. The theme of excess volume of information and literature was apparent in the student comments:

> It becomes a bottomless pit and it's very un-motivating to not know whether you've done something or not, you know, I'm finding that one of the real challenges of my PhD, is that you just don't know whether you've done your work or not, you don't know, you never get to the bottom of anything, you just go round and round in circles and you never really know whether you've done it or not.
>
> *(Sally Interview 3)*

The length of texts was also reported as an issue:

> It's, like, click on the PDF, it could be one page or it could be a thousand pages . . . you just constantly feeling like, you click on something, and then you just think, oh God, I haven't got time to read that and then you close it again, you constantly just sort of thinking, oh God, you know, all the time, so it's just an overload of information I think really.
>
> *(Sally Interview 3)*

Email overload also came up in the data, and the student reported a sense of wasted time and becoming 'bogged down'. Again, this sits in contrast to the notion that technology will inevitably speed up practice and render it more efficient – here the abundance of texts, resources and messages enabled by the technologies was reported as a burden which could slow down progress.

A further theme identified was *keeping up* – with students reporting that they struggled to keep abreast of fast-changing technologies, and new versions of software:

> I felt a bit frustrated . . . 'cause I'm studying here four years ago and I used to use a different version of EndNote. So I was trying to use it the same way now, the new version, and it wasn't working. And I was like why isn't it working, so I felt a bit frustrated because something that used to work in a way now seems to work completely different.
>
> *(PhD Focus Group)*

> When I used Excel the first time – that must have been about 1999. And then the next time I used it was 2010/11, and I thought, you know, it can't have changed that much, I mean, Word still works pretty much the same and it's only changed colour, so it should work, and I was pretty much lost.
>
> *(Frederick Interview 1)*

Students reported that decisions had to be taken as to whether to try to keep up with these changes, or to allow familiarity to lapse. This finding appears to be at odds with the cumulative progress models of digital literacy discussed in Chapter 4. Fluency with technologies did not appear to continue in a smooth upward curve, but instead appeared more varied, with some platforms being allowed to lapse, while others were prioritised. This more 'spiky', contingent and unstable profile of engagement seems poorly theorised by these models, and seems more indicative of the type of assemblage-based, bricolage-style, 'what works' engagement we have seen throughout the data. The students appeared willing to choose a form of 'slowness' if it suited their purposes and priorities, instead of applying themselves to digital technologies in an undifferentiated way. This stance seems reminiscent of the *gambler* orientation (Horning, Ahrens and Gerhard 1999:24) – driven by pragmatism and sensitive to the minutiae of the emerging assemblage.

Intrusion was a further theme, with the ubiquity of networked digital technologies and simultaneous and overlapping nature of engagement being reported as problematic. The expectation that responses to message should be instantaneous was mentioned:

> I feel as though we've become a society that wants everything now, instantaneously. You need to be replying immediately. Not everybody's

able to do that and not everybody wants to do that. And what happened to the once-upon-a-time, you know, you check your email or we didn't even have email, you know, it was a message in your pigeonhole, you know. And now you're bombarded at seven o'clock in the morning. You walk in, you're, like, what? I've got a hundred emails in my, in my, you know, box to go through. And, you know, that can take up a lot of time.

(Master's Focus Group)

Students reported a sense of surveillance. For example, Django reports a sense of pressure to engage with the university virtual learning environment (VLE):

So, I just simply have to be plugged in all the time. But I never started that way, on a Moodle thing, or being online, where, you know, one, everybody sees your conversations, and so I'm finding I'm being really careful about what I'm writing on there, and I don't feel it's a natural conversation then because the, the tutors are always watching and listening. So, I can see the point that, one, yes, they can ... You know, it's an open forum of discussion, but in the other way, that this whole kind of voyeuristic thing with it I find quite frightening.

(Django Interview 1)

This sense that the discussion space could be 'frightening' as well as enabling complicates narratives of student-centred interaction online, which it appears can be regarded as an activity that is under surveillance. In terms of 'entiming', the platform is asynchronous, but the tutor presence is still felt to be ubiquitous.

Students also reported the distractions and temptations of social media throughout their days, such as Frederick:

If I'm working at the computer, because I'm doing my literature review at the moment, so I'll be reading a document, and then sometimes, you know, I might be open for someone to contact me if they want to. Sometimes it gets out of hand and too many people will want to tell me something on Facebook while I'm reading, and then I just, you know, I can't do the task, and then I say, right, my PhD does have some priority, and I'll just say, sorry, I'll have to go offline with Facebook and I turn Facebook off completely.

(Frederick Interview 1)

In this quote and in others in the data, there is a sense that students are actively managing, and seeking to contain, technologies in terms of their time intervals. The simultaneity of all of social media and also academic-related digital platforms and resources, and crucially their availability on the same device, led the students to actively curate their access to what they deemed to be non-academic engagement. Again, this does not accord with the 'anytime, anywhere' notion of simultaneous technologies as empowering – instead we see efforts on the part of the students to protect their time and practices by restricting access to technologies.

A further finding was the extent to which technologies affected the *sequence* and order of activities, for example, visiting the 'analogue' library:

> I never go there (to the library) before I've searched everything online in terms of books and whatever I'm going to get there. I don't go there without having an idea already of what I'm going to get, so I search on their online catalogue first and get, um, every single booklet and everything before I go there.
>
> *(PhD Focus Group)*

Students also reported that the 'entiming' of technologies with the speed of networks could influence the time of day when activities would be undertaken:

> They advise us to use Skype just for the, the chatting bit . . . Not the video bit 'cause that slows it down. And usually it kicks it out after a few minutes if you try . . . it only works right deep at night when no one else is online. That's the best time to do research is between twelve and five in the morning.
>
> *(PhD Focus Group)*

> I've had this problem with Twitter which is time, 'cause usually you follow world time so I, if I go to Twitter during night time it's likely to find your organisation is from the US, same thing. So, it, because I don't, there are so many people and so many things to follow, sometimes it's hard to keep track, so if you're not there in the space of time where they posted something, you miss it.
>
> *(PhD Focus Group)*

Again, in this theme we see how the detail and minutiae of digital engagement is interlaced with situated and particular circumstances and challenges.

The students were also found to be using technologies to *make future time*, in Yuki's case by recording and storage:

> For example, when I attend a lecture or a session I always record the session, and it's after the session, but sometimes I listen to the lecture again to confirm my knowledge or reflect the session . . . when I, for example we're writing an essay and I have to . . . confirm what the lecturer said, I could confirm with the recording data.
>
> *(Yuki Interview 1)*

Juan also refers to how he uses digital technologies to store texts and create reminders, thus also structuring his future time:

> I have articles and after a day or an hour of whatever searching and I've got ten of these and I haven't read them because I haven't got time, what do I do with that? And, again, what I would usually do is save either the documents or, if they're documents and they're PDFs that can save, I'll probably put them on a USB drive. If it's just a, sort of, link, a website or something, I'll email it to myself – so I'll send, you know, a list of ten and email them to myself. The problem is then the next day I'll come in and I'll open up some of them and I'll try and remember what, kind of, thread I was working off before and, invariably, just start a new one.
>
> *(Juan Interview 3)*

As with space, the student accounts indicate that time was also an active agential presence to be worked with, as opposed to a smooth context. The students describe how they moulded and adjusted their engagement in response to time itself, and also that digital technologies led to a sense of slowing down in addition to speeding up. In this regard, time, like space, can be theorised as an active and complex component in these assemblages.

Conclusions

Throughout this analysis, we argue that technologies do not provide an 'escape' from either space or time, but instead they are entangled with both in complex ways. In this regard, space and time can be seen as further agents in the assemblages that formed the site of engagement, with constant, emergent negotiation taking place in terms of agency and practice. These assemblages are both constituted by space and time and also constitutive of spatiality and the 'entiming' of practice and engagement. The complexities and dilemmas that these capacities generate are striking and, throughout, the student accounts reveal the highly situated and specific nature of these assemblages, with space and time as active agents. This takes us a step further in our attempt to resituate and explore student engagement in the digital university. In the next chapter, we will look in more detail at how these messy, and at times challenging, assemblages unfold.

References

Adam, E. 1995. *Timewatch: The Social Analysis of Time.* Cambridge: Polity Press.
Adam, E. 2004. *Time.* London: Wiley.
Adam, B. 2006. Time, *Theory, Culture and Society* 23(2-3), 119–126.
Augé, M. 1995. *Non-Places: Introduction to an Anthropology of Supermodernity.* London: Verso.

Clark, H. 2002. *Building Education: The Role of the Physical Environment in Enhancing Teaching and Research*. London: Institute of Education, University of London.

Finkelstein, A., Ferris, J., Winer, L. and Weston, C. 2014. *Principles for Designing Teaching and Learning Spaces*. Montreal: Teaching and Learning Services, McGill University.

Gourlay, L. 2014. Creating time: students, technologies and temporal practices in higher education. *E-Learning and Digital Media* 11(2), 141–153.

Gourlay, L. and Oliver, M. 2016. Students' physical and digital sites of study: making, marking and breaking boundaries. In L. Carvalho, P. Goodyear and M. de Laat (Eds.), *Place-Based Spaces for Networked Learning*. London: Routledge, 77–92.

Gourlay, L., Oliver, M. and Lanclos, D. 2015. Sociomaterial texts, spaces and devices: questioning 'digital dualism' in library and study practices. *Higher Education Quarterly* 69(3), 263–278.

Grosz, E. 2004. *The Nick of Time: Politics, Evolution and the Untimely*. Durham, NC: Duke University Press.

Hamilton, S. and Zimmerman, J. 2002. Breaking through zero-sum academics: two students' perspectives on computer-mediated learning environments. In K. Rudestram and J. Schoenholtz-Read (Eds.), *The Handbook of Online Learning Innovations in Higher Education and Corporate Training*. London: SAGE.

Hannam, K., Sheller, M. and Urry, J. 2006. Editorial: mobilities, immobilities and moorings. *Mobilities* 1(1), 1–22.

Hayles, N. K. 1996. Embodied virtuality: or how to put bodies back in the picture. In M. Moser and D. MacLeod (Eds.), *Immersed in Technology*. Cambridge, MA: MIT Press, 1–28.

Hayles, N. K. 1999. *How We Became Posthuman*. London: University of Chicago Press.

Hiltz, S. R. and Wellman, B. 1997. Asynchronous learning networks as a virtual classroom. *Communications of the ACM* 40(9), 44–49.

Horning, K., Ahrens, D. and Gerhard, A. 1999. Do technologies have time? New practices of time and the transformation of communication technologies. *Time and Society* 8(2–3), 293–308.

JISC. 2006. *Designing Spaces for Effective Learning: A Guide to 21st Century Learning Design*. http://webarchive.nationalarchives.gov.uk/20140703004833/http://www.jisc.ac.uk/media/documents/publications/learningspaces.pdf [Accessed 10 Aug 2017].

Knox, J. 2013. Five critiques of the open educational resources movement. *Teaching in Higher Education* 18(8), 821–832.

Land, R. 2005. Embodiment and risk in cyberspace education. In R. Land and S. Bayne (Eds.), *Education in Cyberspace*. London: Routledge, 149–164.

Latour, B. 2004. Why has critique run out of steam? From matters of fact to matters of concern. *Critical Inquiry* 30(2), 225–248.

Lemke, J. 2000. Metamedia literacy: transforming meanings and media. In D. Reinking, M. McKenna, L. Labbo and R. Kieffer (Eds.), *Handbook of Literacy and Technology: Transformations in a Post-Typographic World*. Hillsdale, NJ: Lawrence Erlbaum, 283–302.

Massey, D. 2005. *For Space*. London: SAGE.

Monaghan, T. 2002. Flexible space and built pedagogy: emerging IT embodiments. *Inventio* 4(1), 1–19.

Temple, P. 2007. *Learning Spaces for the 21st Century: A Review of the Literature*. York: Higher Education Academy.

UCISA. 2016. *The UK Higher Education Learning Space Toolkit*. www.ucisa.ac.uk/learningspace [Accessed 13 Jul 2017].

Urry, J. 2007. *Mobilities*. Cambridge: Polity Press.

9

FLUID ASSEMBLAGES AND RESILIENCE

Although students are frequently presented as being fluent users of digital technologies, the previous chapters have shown that things can be much more complicated. If we cannot rely on sweeping generational discourses to reassure us that current learners are digital natives, for whom technology use is natural and desirable, we must instead face the possibility that there will be times when students struggle with the technologies that we require them to use.

This was seen earlier, in Chapter 6, where students' orientations towards technologies included both 'combat' and 'coping', as well as the more fluent experience of 'curating'. This chapter will explore these moments of struggle further and explore what can be done to support students. This exploration will draw in the concept of educational resilience.

What is Resilience?

Resilience is an appealing concept that has been studied in several different contexts and under a series of different names. It has parallels, for example, with the psychological concept of 'grit', which has been explored in US contexts (Duckworth and Gross 2014) – although it does not necessarily have the same longitudinal scope or scale. Similarly, it relates to Barnett's ideas about the 'fragility' of students' will to learn (24–25), including the importance of self-belief on both their persistence and the quality of their learning; the value that students can derive from supportive others (58–59); and the kinds of risk-averse pedagogies that can limit students' capacity to use challenges as opportunities for development (143–145) (Barnett 2007). Ross, Gallagher and Macleod (2013) also referred to the idea of resilience in their work on students' retention and completion. In that work, they defined it as 'the ability to navigate conditions of complexity and change. In practice, in this context, this mostly means that the student keeps going and successfully achieves the qualification sought' (Ross, Gallagher and Macleod 2013:52).

Early accounts of resilience emerged in fields such as medicine to explain the apparent psychological 'invulnerability' of exceptional individuals within populations to conditions such as coronary disease (Waxman, Gray and Padrón 2004:41). Sociologically, the idea was taken up because it proved useful in explaining how individuals who were *vulnerable* – exposed to poverty, biological risks, and family instability, and reared by parents with little education or serious mental health problems – [. . .] remained *invincible* and developed into competent and autonomous young adults' (Werner and Smith 1982:3).

Educational interest in resilience emerged as a response to previous work that had categorised demographic groups of learners as being systematically 'at risk' – for example, from poverty, drug use or sexual abuse, or though physical or mental impairment. These categories were originally identified through their association with poor educational outcomes, but ended up carrying deterministic connotations for policymakers and researchers. The consequence of this was that the groups identified as at risk were treated as being inevitably in deficit. Against this fatalistic backdrop, the idea of educational resilience provided a way of explaining how individuals might succeed in spite of these 'environmental factors' (Brown 2004, Howard, Dryden and Johnson 1999).

Part of the usefulness of this concept was that, at the time of these discussions, policy-driven interventions typically promoted risk avoidance. This reduced the prevalence of problems, but also limited opportunities. By contrast, initiatives focused on developing educational resilience promoted understanding, informed decision-making and cultivated behaviours associated with success.

> The resiliency perspective [. . .] may help us design more effective educational interventions because it enables us to specifically identify those 'alterable' factors that distinguish resilient and nonresilient students. [. . .] The construct of 'educational resilience' is not viewed as a fixed attribute of some students, but rather as alterable processes or mechanisms that can be developed and fostered. In other words, this approach does not focus on attributes such as ability, because ability has not been found to be characteristic of resilient students.
>
> *(Waxman, Gray and Padrón 2004:4)*

Instead of being determined by attributes, educational resilience was best explained in terms of learned behaviours that developed supportive relationships, high expectations (of the self and by others), and access to supportive resources (including people and things that could sustain studying). Examples that illustrate this include studies of 'turnaround teachers' who were pivotal in cases where at-risk students overcame the educational challenges they faced (Waxman, Gray and Padrón 2004).

These individuals raised expectations, provided encouragement and support and also contributed to the creation of environments conducive to studying. However, even the presence of such individuals is no guarantee of success. This led researchers to move further away from an 'environmental factors' view of development and towards more agentive definitions of educational resilience, such as 'a person's ability to adjust or be adaptable and successful in an academic setting' (Barone 2004:87).

Fluid Entanglements

The development of the idea of educational resilience has swung away from the idea of invulnerable individuals, across to the consideration of environmental factors that might determine success, and back to a position in which individuals act upon and react to the environments in which they are operating in order to achieve their goals. This later conception, in which the agency of individuals emerges as a consequence of the people and things with which they interact, brings educational resilience close to sociomaterial accounts and to the influence of the 'wash of material stuff and spaces' on educational success (Fenwick, Edwards and Sawchuk 2011:vii).

As shown in the previous chapters, successful studying involves the co-ordination of people, things, spaces and times. The orientations of combat and coping described in Chapter 6 show, further, that even when studying is successful, this co-ordination can be a struggle. Sometimes, the elements of networks resist incorporation (like the networked printer in Faith's common room), or act in unexpected ways (like the algorithms that placed targeted adverts alongside Sally's email inbox). An important principle in ANT is that the same analysis that is used to explain success should also be able to explain failure (Callon 1984). As such, the same analysis that was used in earlier chapters to explore students' routine study practices should also be able to explain ruptures and breakdowns, and, importantly for this chapter, how assemblages then develop further. Breakdowns are particularly important in sociomaterial analyses: they make visible the ways in which taken-for-granted elements (be they people or things) are needed for this to happen.

> Objects, no matter how important, efficient, central, or necessary they may be, tend to recede into the background [. . . until revealed by] accidents, breakdowns, and strikes: all of a sudden, completely silent intermediaries become full- blown mediators; even objects, which a minute before appeared fully automatic, autonomous, and devoid of human agents, are now made of crowds of frantically moving humans with heavy equipment. Those who watched the Columbia shuttle instantly transformed from the most complicated human instrument ever assembled to a rain of debris falling over Texas will realize how quickly objects flip-flop their mode of existence.
>
> *(Latour 2005:81)*

This dual analysis, where an exceptional moment reveals the components of ongoing success that have been taken for granted, can be seen across the experiences of the students who took part in our study. Some ways in which assemblages developed after such moments will be illustrated in the sections that follow.

Changes Involving Nonhuman Actors

Sometimes, the breakdowns that took place involved the students' relationship with specific technologies. These included commonplace challenges like forgetting passwords or having to work with updated versions of software they had once been familiar with. Faith, for example, explained that the schools where she was working on placement for her PGCE often had older versions of Microsoft Office than she used as a student, and that she had learned to save copies of her files in older formats to ensure that they would work when she took them into schools.

Moving past these moments of breakdown involved avoiding these problematic relationships. Commonly, this involved un-enrolling the problematic technology from the assemblage and enrolling some alternative instead. Sally, for example, described her struggles with referencing software and how she eventually worked with an alternative technology.

> When I did my MSc I used EndNote Web, and after the initial novelty of it had worn off, I realised it was actually really crap, and it has loads of bugs in it and it is really, really, annoying. It has a lot of bugs in it, and it tries to, kind of, cover every possible eventuality and it just doesn't do it very well [. . .] it just gives you all the wrong fields, it puts, like, capital letters in the wrong places. [. . .] Partly I put it down to the fact that it was EndNote Web was free, and I thought they probably make it crap, the free version so you'll go and buy the real one, and then when I started doing my PhD I actually got the proper EndNote put on my computer and realised that it was no different, it's still just as crap and still just as annoying, you have to do, like, endless workarounds. [. . .] So, I was starting to get absolutely frustrated with EndNote Web, I was finding it really difficult to synchronise the version that sat on the computer with the version on the web, like the back-up of what they use on the web, the cloud, and I just found the whole, I was literally tearing my hair out with it and getting nowhere. And then I went to a seminar that was run by a member of our department, and they were talking, she talked about Zotero. [. . .] So I decided to transfer to Zotero, which I did, and I imported all my references and I did find Zotero to be better in a lot of ways.
>
> *(Sally Interview 4)*

From a sociomaterial perspective, resilience in this case relates to the fluidity of the assemblage (de Laet and Mol 2000): it remains recognisable as Sally's study practices, even though it has been reconfigured. A further, more involved, part of this resilience was the work involved in recovering rather than losing resources – specifically, the way Sally was able to recover existing work by extricating references from one platform and importing them into the other. This workaround was not purely a technical matter, and nor was it purely a result of Sally's agency – for example, she found out about Zotero from someone in her department. In this case, however, the problem was resolved by disentangling one element of the network and incorporating a new one, illustrating the fluid, improvised way in which such practices can be sustained.

Sometimes, the breakdowns were severe enough that substitutions were not enough to resolve them. In these cases, rather than minor modifications or substitutions, it was sometimes necessary to shore up the assemblage by adding new things into the network. This increase in complexity extended the network, illustrating its fluidity, but starting to test whether or not this is recognisably the same assemblage – whether it was still possible to trace the materiality of this assemblage as an immutable mobile (Latour 2005:226). In the examples here, the continuity of students' reported experiences is important: it signals that, for them at least, this was still the same assemblage, even if its components had changed and it had grown more complicated.

One important and recurrent example of this growth in complexity was the ongoing challenge all students faced of how many supporting texts they should bring in to support their argument when writing assessed work. Here, even if individual drafts were clearly different, there was important continuity in the way that this was experienced as the 'same' essay.

However, in some cases, bringing in new technologies allowed problems to be solved by splitting one network into parallel structures, and here the breakdowns did result in discontinuities in the assemblage – arguably, these examples suggest that the old and new practices, although related, were no longer versions of the same immutable mobile. Sally, for example, described how the separation of email into different accounts, each one kept on a separate device, enabled her to manage the way in which Google's algorithms parsed her email and profiled her.

> I've come to terms with it slightly now. I've found a way to manage the little bugger, which is that I created another Gmail account which I don't get email to, and this other Gmail account is just for the purposes of the phone. So now the phone thinks that I am [string of letters and numbers] blah, blah, blah @ gmail.com, when actually there are no emails that ever go to . . . well, there might be, I never look at things like junk mail anyway, so . . . And then, I then do things like I back my contacts up to that Gmail account, and then actually my Gmail is another one. So that's the way I've managed to manage it at the moment, because I just wasn't happy about the intrusiveness of it.
>
> *(Sally Interview 1)*

In these kinds of cases, students had to weigh up the relative effort of enrolling new elements into the assemblage against the possible outcomes they might then be able to achieve, and whether this would require the creation of additional assemblages rather than just modifications of the existing ones. Time and money exerted particularly visible influences on these adaptations.

> I think for a lot of students obviously, you know, the degree itself is quite a serious investment. [. . .] I'll find a document or article and then just use Google to find maybe a pre-publication copy. That's something I never knew existed before doing this course, and that's really quite useful. [Interviewer: How did you find out about that?] I really don't know, basically stinginess. I think that's what it is, you know. I probably found a document, and it was like you're going to have to pay to get access to this document, and I was like oh that's quite a lot of money for it, and I don't even know if it is any good. So, I don't really want to pay. So, then I will use Google to try and find it some other way. And in doing that, you know, you actually find that the internet is full of crazy information, you know. Locating the information is the difficult thing, but there's so much out there.
>
> *(Bokeh Interview 1)*

Changes Involving Human Actors

A closely related pattern of recovery involved changing students' relationships with other people. Sally, for example, expressed concern about the security of using her phone's mobile data as a hotspot for her laptop. She could not resolve this technically, so resorted to a social solution:

> My laptop is so old, but when I use portable hotspot on my phone it cannot be secure, so in other words it doesn't have that, like, you know, the symbol of the lock. So, what that means is it's because the encryption technology has gone beyond what my laptop can do . . . so basically what it means is that anybody . . . If I put the hotspot on my mobile, it means other people around in the vicinity could potentially use my bandwidth. So, I made a scary sounding name hoping to keep people from using my signal. [Interviewer reads from the image: Trojan Horseman? Excellent.] [. . .] I just thought that would, like, put people off and it's got, like, this scary zero that I put in. This is how I deal with technology. This is, like, the way I am. I have to invent all these, like, ridiculous things to, sort of, get around . . . [. . .] It's the equivalent of, like, gaffer tape basically; it's all held together with nothing. So trojanh0rseman . . .
>
> *(Sally Interview 2)*

The inclusion of the 'scary zero' was a reference to 'leetspeak', which involves the substitution of visually similar characters for alphabetic letters – something developed on bulletin board systems in the 1980s and associated with communities of hackers. Since Sally could not disentangle the technology she relied on from her existing network, the alternative involved entangling undesirables, associating her study setup with groups that others might find off-putting, so that they would not look too closely at whether or not they could exploit it.

Just as some breakdowns could only be resolved by increasing the complexity of the assemblage by adding nonhuman actors, other breakdowns required the addition of human actors. Several participants identified challenges that they had faced – often technical, but sometimes educational – where they had not been able to resolve the matter by themselves. At this point, other people sometimes got involved to strengthen the assemblage. These included fellow students, professionals with more experience, or even just friends and family.

> [Interviewer: Did you get any guidance or training to help you?] No, only – how can I say? – apprenticeship: ask others, ask a senior [professional]. When I could travel with something, PC seems to break down, or I couldn't deal with this data. When always we have to ask someone who knows, because there was no internet website. Now we can afford us of this kind of internet site. We can ask something, everyone in all over the world, but at that time we have to ask someone we know, some friends or colleagues.
>
> *(Yuki Interview 1)*

Louise described something similar. She had experienced a problem with a computer virus, and in this case, it was her mother's support network that was eventually able to rebuild things for her.

> I was on the TES website so really reliable, the main website looking at resources and it really seems that I got this to computer virus from one of those resources which is so peculiar, but yes, basically I thought that my laptop was going to be dead forever. It wiped everything, but my mum took it into the IT department at her school where she works and the guy managed to save it which was very kind of him, and I guess in terms of talking about kind of different spaces that was quite kind that like my mum took it into her school and they kind of fixed it when it wasn't anything, it wasn't their work at all.
>
> *(Louise Interview 3)*

Again, these examples show how fluid assemblages could be. In these cases, new people and things join the network; importantly, they might also withdraw later, once their support is no longer needed to keep things working.

Changes Involving Human and Nonhuman Actors

Obviously, there were also cases in which both human and nonhuman elements were involved in strengthening the network – as was the case with Juan's library.

> I use the [institution's] computers because they're often free, and, you know, I quite like using them, but the trouble is to get . . . if I find something that's actually very useful and I want to print, at the [institution] you can't print double-sided, so it's quite . . . it's more expensive. So, I go to [a different institution nearby] and use my girlfriend's password on the computers there and print. And so, I then have to change, so I spend quite a . . . more time going between libraries if I want to print something.
>
> *(Juan Interview 2)*

Here, the financial challenges that Juan faced were overcome through the involvement of his girlfriend, her ID and password, and the computer network and printers of a second institution. Although this made the network that enabled his studying more complicated, these elements were easier for him to enrol than securing extra funding would be, and were reliable enough to be trusted parts of the assemblage.

Times and Spaces

As well as the human and nonhuman actors discussed above, some breakdowns involved changes in time and space. Although analytically, these might be understood as nonhuman actors, they are drawn out separately here so that their agency is recognised and they are not treated as background or context, as discussed in Chapter 8.

Yuki experienced problems with Wi-Fi, problems which were overcome by associating study with specific times. Tasks that required internet access were aligned with the brief periods when the service was reliable enough.

> Average day, 90 per cent I write in my room from the morning, because Wi-Fi access is very poor in my room, except for early in the morning. So, I need to get up before six, and from . . . yes, before eight o'clock, it is very good, Wi-Fi access is very good. So, I mean, I . . . For example, downloading some materials from [the virtual learning environment], or something like that, I have to down before eight o'clock, and then start writing or reading.
>
> *(Yuki Interview 3)*

The issues involving time that arose were often to do with too many people seeking to use the same resource simultaneously – whether that was Wi-Fi, or a particular book or a particularly nice desk in the library. This shows a slightly different kind of fluidity in the development of assemblages: sometimes, they fluctuated, adapted and reappeared in predictable rhythms, shaped by the way that they intersected with others.

Educational Resilience as a Matter of Care

The analysis above shows the kinds of growth and fluidity that students described in their study assemblages, explaining resilience in terms of the adaptation of heterogeneous networks. However, if our analysis of studying takes place at the level of these networks, this raises questions for educators and others who might wish to make a difference to individual students. How can a person be helped if we are required to understand them in terms of the varied networks they are involved with at different times?

One approach to resolving this involves thinking about students using Latour's analysis of matters of concern. Early studies using Actor-Network Theory explored how scientific knowledge was produced, showing how social and political concerns were inextricably bound up with scientific work (Latour and Woolgar 1979). Facts, it was argued, depend on the instruments that measure, the technologies that transcribe, the materials that are consumed and the people who manage, manipulate, write about and discuss these processes. As a consequence, instead of attending to facts in isolation or attributing causal power to them as if they acted alone, it is important to understand the circumstances and means through which they were produced and are maintained.

> When we list the qualities of an ANT account, we will make sure that when agencies are introduced, they are never *presented* simply as matters of fact, but always as *matters of concern*, with their mode of fabrication and their stabilizing mechanisms clearly visible.
>
> *(Latour 2005:120)*

Superficially, this might look like a tactic to undermine scientific knowledge. It has certainly been used politically to call into doubt the credibility of inconvenient scientific claims, such as those around climate change, by emphasising the social interests that shaped their production (Latour 2004). However, Latour's contention is that all facts are constituted in this way. Some are stronger than others, however. This means that particular claims may need ongoing work to maintain them, because 'if something is constructed, then it means it is fragile and thus in great need of care and caution' (Latour 2004:246).

This was developed further by Puig de la Bellacasa (2011) and others, through a discussion of matters of care, which draws attention to the ongoing work required to stabilise matters. This work involves practices of caring for things and constitutes affective as well as practical labour; it is a world-making process that involves acknowledging and engaging with conflicting positions to our own, and which necessarily draws attention to the kinds of arrangements researchers (and others) are working to support, and which they are not. The work involves strengthening matters by adding layers of concern – building up new associations and new connections that secure and reinforce what is there. Such strengthening requires attention to weaknesses and limits: caring requires challenging specific assemblages and paying attention to who or what has been excluded, and why (*ibid.* 96).

Treating educational resilience as a matter of care requires testing the limits of successful practice, focusing on points of struggle and exclusion, and engaging with these particular sociotechnical assemblages in order to understand what labour has been taken for granted, what things have been neglected and what new relationships could be built. The building and stabilising of these new relationships draws in a third idea from Actor-Network Theory: punctualisation, the creation of a 'black box' where an assemblage can be relied upon to operate as if it were a single, integrated actor, object or institution (Law 1992). These black boxes are always precarious – be they a television, government or human body – each can degenerate into a complex and messy assemblage as parts fail or relationships break down, as shown earlier with Latour's quote about the Columbia shuttle. However, while they work, they can be treated as resources, which can be drawn upon quickly and relatively easily in ways that can be reproduced.

To draw on Bowker and Star (1999), when things can be punctualised in this way and can be drawn on successfully over time, they become taken for granted and invisible: they become part of the infrastructure on which subsequent action can depend. The challenge for the institution, then, becomes provision of infrastructure: things and people that are easy to find and incorporate into networks of study practices, or which actively reach out to the student to offer assistance or intervene at points of difficulty.

Examples of Infrastructure

The participants' interviews identified many things that fit this definition of infrastructure, in that they operate as stable black boxes so that students can take them for granted without having to understand or repair them. Some of these were simply on hand if needed, like the collection of resources in the library; others made themselves known more actively, like the reminders of Wi-Fi connectivity that popped up on students' phones.

The participants also identified several things that ought to operate as infrastructure but did not. In some cases, the same technology worked as a black box for some students but not for others, illustrating how qualities are not fixed, but emerge from interactions across networks. As an example of the kind of thing that might count as infrastructure, most students were able to rely on the digital collection held by the library. Many, but not all, could rely on their institutional email accounts. The exceptions here included students whose mailbox size exceeded their quota (so that they were no longer able to receive new emails), and those who relied on personal or professional email accounts (so failed to check their institutional email regularly enough to receive the updates they needed). Virtual learning environments also formed part of the infrastructure for most but not all of the students. Problems included issues of usability and, more commonly, passwords. In some cases, it was the interaction of pieces of infrastructure that caused issues, so that even though each individual part operated more or less as it should, they became problematic when combined.

> Part of the reason why I don't check the [institutional] email as frequently is that it's a bit of a, um, it's lengthy process to get into it from remote access because you have to go into, like, the [institutional] website, then into [the virtual learning environment], and then you have to log in again.
>
> *(PGCE Focus Group)*

Here, the difficulties of access, co-ordinating digital identities with access to information, systematically left this student without information that would have helped their studies.

From the perspective of matters of care, institutional developments could have improved the experience for this student, treating the poorly co-ordinated institutional services as components and 'black boxing' them further, so that the student could associate the services more easily with their networks of study, strengthening and adding these new associations to the assemblages they worked with. One way to do this was through the development of a single sign-on service. This now allows the student's ID and password to be entered once; the login credentials are then passed to the institution's other systems so that the student does not need to manage multiple logins. Creating this has made it simpler for students to adopt a whole range of institutional systems.

An even simpler development of institutional infrastructure would have solved the problems Juan faced in the earlier example. To recap, Juan chose to use another library rather than spend more money on printing articles single sided. In this case, the network administrator could have opened the black box of the printing settings, allowing students greater choice about how to use the printers. Enabling double-sided printing would have allowed the complex network of spaces, digital identities and documents that Juan worked with to be replaced by a simple selection from a drop-down menu and a mouse click.

What these simple examples illustrate is how students looked for systems and services to be simple, stable and easy to co-opt into their activities. Systems that were also active enough to remind students they were there were even more useful. When students faced educational challenges – as small as printing a note or as large as writing a thesis – they inevitably had to improvise; the assemblages that enabled their studying were fluid, and adapted on an ongoing basis to ensure that the right kinds of entanglements with people and things were present. The imperative for the institution was to make these potential components as easy to find and enrol as possible;

for example, by creating services that signalled their availability to students, so that the students' effort could be spent on the end of pursuing their goal, rather than on building the assemblage that formed the means for their task.

As with the earlier examples of educational resilience, the burden of making a service stable so that it is easy to incorporate can involve social as well as technical elements. It has been clear for some decades that making technical systems robust involves 'configuring the user' to become a 'good' user by training and guiding them about how they are expected to behave, as well as by adapting the system itself (Grint and Woolgar 1997). This process was also visible here. So, for example, learning about various digital resources in a timely manner helped students to create the assemblages that they needed. Faith, for example, described how important it was when starting to use unfamiliar software to be able to 'see the demo first, and later on to try and do some practical things by myself, to see if I can manage' (Faith Interview 1). Other students made reference to guides, videos or turning to peers for advice about how to use particular services or resources. All of these became mediating actors, helping to configure these users so that the students were able to associate these resources with their established networks more easily.

However, not all students struggled with the same things, and so it is important to recognise that configurations which work for one person might cause problems for another. For example, Laura reported finding the virtual classes that she took part in using Elluminate to be very positive. She found them

> . . . very simple and I felt very safe in that environment. I didn't feel threatened or anything. What is, what I find interesting is that they do all the sessions with no video so we don't see each other. [. . .] It does enable you to start kind of talking, to raise your hand, and I don't know, maybe it's less threatening.
>
> *(Laura Interview 1)*

By contrast, one of the participants in the focus group for online students commented on how much they valued the use of the video. They compared their Elluminate classes with Skype, saying that 'for the first time I was seeing one of the members of the group and it just put things in a different perspective' (Online Student Focus Group). Again, this illustrates the point that the qualities of these resources are not fixed, but instead emerge from their relationships with the other elements with which they are entangled.

Conclusions

It is a common criticism that research into educational technology can be celebratory and uncritical (e.g. Selwyn 2011). An account of how students succeed in their studies should also be able to explain breakdowns and ruptures, and the ongoing processes of improvisation and repair that give assemblages continuity.

The idea of educational resilience provides a useful perspective on students' study practices, recognising that these can be difficult to maintain and that many students experience struggles in their studies. Rethinking educational resilience from a sociomaterial perspective connects this idea to wider debates about materiality, showing how assemblages of resources, technologies, places and other people can be sustained. This draws attention to the fluidity of study practices and the way that these assemblages are constantly renegotiated and adapted as the demands on students change. Studying might involve many stable patterns, but it also involves improvisation and maintenance work.

Across all of this, the institution has an important role to play. It, too, consists of material elements as well as social ones. Its responsibilities towards students can be met, in part, by ensuring that the resources and services that they need are visible and stable, and even that they act to provide students with support instead of waiting to be incorporated. From a sociomaterial perspective, this becomes a matter of care: we can support learners by strengthening the assemblages they are part of so that these are secured, adapted or extended. This requires the creation of a reliable infrastructure which can be incorporated into the entanglements of people and things that are necessary for studying. In the next chapter, we will go on to look at how institutions themselves develop, and the ways in which new policies or services can improve students' experiences – or undermine them.

References

Barnett, R. 2007. *Will to Learn: Being a Student in an Age of Uncertainty*. New York: McGraw-Hill Education.

Barone, D. 2004. A longitudinal look at the literacy development of children prenatally exposed to crack/cocaine. In H. Waxman, Y. Padrón and J. Gray (Eds.), *Educational Resiliency: Student, Teacher and School Perspectives*. Greenwich, CO: Information Age Publishing, 87–112.

Bowker, G. and Star, S. 1999. *Sorting Things Out: Classification and its Consequences*. Cambridge, MA: MIT Press.

Brown, J. 2004. Resilience: emerging social constructions in educational policy, research, and practice. In H. Waxman, Y. Padrón and J. Gray (Eds.), *Educational Resiliency: Student, Teacher and School Perspectives*. Greenwich, CO: Information Age Publishing, 11–36.

Callon, M. 1984. Some elements of a sociology of translation: domestication of the scallops and the fishermen of St Brieuc Bay. *The Sociological Review* 32(1), 196–233.

De Laet, M. and Mol, A. (2000). The Zimbabwe bush pump: mechanics of a fluid technology. *Social Studies of Science* 30(2), 225–263.

Duckworth, A. and Gross, J. 2014. Self-control and grit: related but separable determinants of success. *Current Directions in Psychological Science* 23(5), 319–325.

Fenwick, T., Edwards, R. and Sawchuk, P. 2011. *Emerging Approaches to Educational Research: Tracing the Sociomaterial*. London: Routledge.

Grint, K. and Woolgar, S. 1997. *The Machine at Work: Technology, Work and Organization*. Cambridge: Polity Press.

Howard, S., Dryden, J. and Johnson, B. 1999. Childhood resilience: review and critique of literature. *Oxford Review of Education* 25(3), 307–323.

Latour, B. 2004. Why has critique run out of steam? From matters of fact to matters of concern. *Critical Inquiry* 30(2), 225–248.

Latour, B. 2005. *Reassembling the Social: An Introduction to Actor-Network-Theory*. Oxford: Oxford University Press.

Latour, B. and Woolgar, S. 1979. *Laboratory Life: The Social Construction of Scientific Facts*. Beverly Hills: SAGE.

Law, J. 1992. Notes on the theory of the actor-network: ordering, strategy, and heterogeneity. *Systemic Practice and Action Research* 5(4), 379–393.

Puig de la Bellacasa, M. 2011. Matters of care in technoscience: assembling neglected things. *Social Studies of Science* 41(1), 85–106.

Ross, J., Gallagher, M. and Macleod, H. 2013. Making distance visible: assembling nearness in an online distance learning programme. *International Review of Research in Online and Distance Learning* 14(4), 51–66.

Selwyn, N. 2011. In praise of pessimism—the need for negativity in educational technology. *British Journal of Educational Technology* 42(5), 713–718.

Waxman, H., Gray, J. and Padrón, Y. 2004. Promoting educational resilience for students at risk of failure. In H. Waxman, Y. Padrón and J. Gray (Eds.), *Educational Resiliency: Student, Teacher and School Perspectives*. Greenwich, CO: Information Age Publishing, 37–62.

Werner, E. and Smith, R. 1982. *Vulnerable but Invincible: A Longitudinal Study of Resilient Children and Youth*. New York: McGraw-Hill.

10

THE ORGANISATION AS ASSEMBLAGE

The preceding chapters have explored how students engaged, and they have drawn attention to the importance of material considerations such as artefacts and spaces. In Chapter 9, we explored the importance of infrastructure in supporting students' practices through our discussion of educational resilience from a sociomaterial perspective. However, the relationship between the organisation and student practices was a two-way one; students also influenced the organisation, including through the actions of the project. In this chapter, we explore the relationship between the project's work and the host institution in order to analyse what might commonly be described as 'impact'. We will explore how change within organisations has been discussed in the literature, before moving on to look at ways in which the project exerted an influence on the organisation, and how its work influenced decisions about institutional policy and infrastructure.

Impact

Universities across the world are now expected to be 'efficient' and accountable, able to justify the research funding they receive in terms of 'value for money', demonstrated by an evaluation of research volume, quality and impact (Geuna and Martin 2003). Although volume can be measured in various ways, quality and impact are much harder to evaluate – particularly, although not exclusively, in education and other social sciences (Oancea 2013). However, the challenge has been raised that educational researchers could and should do more to engage policymakers and practitioners, and to undertake more of the 'translation' work that might link research to practice (Francis 2011). As Eynon observes,

> 'Impacts' are wide-ranging and often subtle, diffuse and difficult to measure. In reality, our activities are not easily translatable or directly aligned with the kinds of impact that are currently being required from academia to prove the worth of our endeavours. It is perhaps the matching of our 'everyday' impacts with the 'required' impacts where the heart of the challenge lies.
>
> *(Eynon 2012:1)*

Organisation as Technological Effect

As we saw in Chapter 5, much research in the field of educational technology has an instrumental orientation, aligned with managerial discourses of effectiveness and efficiency. This holds true for discussions of the impact of technology on policies and organisations. Research in TEL that has addressed this relationship has typically adopted a rational command-and-control model, treating the complexities of the lived experiences of students and staff as 'noise' in the system that needs to be controlled.

As considered in Chapter 2, discussions of educational technology are rife with myths about transformation. Deterministic models of change dominate discussions (Oliver 2011), for example, in the way that MOOCs were described as an impending 'avalanche', poised to sweep away established models of Higher Education provision (Barber *et al.* 2013), or as a form of 'soft' determinism through the comparisons with industries that have reshaped themselves around new media platforms, such as newspapers and music publishing (Weller 2011).

This utopian thinking, shaped by fantasies about the power of technology, overstates the transformative potential of technology and underplays continuities, resulting in an ideological account of change, as discussed in Chapter 2. Much recent work in this vein draws inspiration from Christensen's exploration of disruptive technologies (Christensen 2013). These are technologies that might result in worse performance – in contrast to sustaining technologies, which improve the performance of established products – but that might be cheaper, or have properties that appeal to a new market, or that can become a platform for accelerated development in the longer term. Christensen's argument is that when businesses fail to invest in disruptive technologies, they risk being overtaken by competitors.

This logic has been applied to universities, suggesting that the scaling up of provision means that while universities focus on growth and efficiency, alternative providers offering online degrees threaten their security, although Christensen and Eyring (2011) do also note that experiences at the best universities are not merely down to the efficient delivery of courses. These concessions open up the space for other discussions about the relationship between technology and change.

Organisation as Tool

Not all debates about technology position the organisation as helpless in the face of technological change. However, the alternative position is not necessarily any more persuasive, tending to present organisations as if they were tools, guided purely by the logic of efficiency, leading to two extreme positions on agency reminiscent of those attributed to students as discussed in Chapter 3.

For example, early accounts treated institutions like machines, using the metaphor of 're-engineering' and recommending Fordist approaches to improve efficiency in a managerial, command-and-control manner, using techniques such as mission statements, measurable targets, performance monitoring, central control of budgets and 'an unbroken chain of responsibility' (Brown 2002:242). It did not take long for problems with this kind of approach to be identified, however. Subsequent work criticised these 'over-simplistic approaches', noting that 'to date, much of the focus has been into the development of technologies or top-down policy aspirations, and not on the human dimensions, scaling up and embedding of innovation and the associated management of change' (Salmon 2005:205). Salmon's alternative, which involves mapping technologies and pedagogies against the strategic objectives of the institution, acknowledges the influences of cultures on change – for example, in terms of the wide variations that exist between disciplines. Nevertheless, the focus remains on planned, top-down change, even if that change is planned to take account of local variations.

There have been more nuanced developments since, however. For example, Sharpe, Benfield and Francis (2006) go slightly further by recognising 'the groundswell of energy and good practice already occurring' (138), promising dialogue and committing support for the development of communities who might implement new ideas. Their approach introduces the idea of contextualisation, suggesting finally that top-down approaches may be inadequate as a way of explaining how institutions change.

Even where there is a more nuanced account of the process of change, the motivation is commonly instrumental, focusing on questions of cost and scale, for example. Salmon (2005) notes how much interest in new technologies is driven by a naïve belief in its economic benefits, but she goes on to discuss innovation in terms of costs and benefits, proposing a framework that relates 'technology and pedagogy' to 'market, mission and objectives'. Laurillard (2007), focusing on issues of sustainability and scaling up education, went further to develop a quantifiable model of the costs of different teaching approaches. This has allowed the development of costing tools and resource appraisal models (Kennedy *et al.* 2015), focusing on major areas of cost such as staff time, and weighing this against quantified profiles of the pedagogies of courses.

Organisations as Assemblages

Actor-Network Theory proposes that scale is a network effect, and that the same principles can be applied to understand why one particular network appears 'bigger' than another, and what their structural effects might be (Latour 2005). As such, this analysis should be able to explain the ongoing production and maintenance of organisations such as universities just as well as it explains study practices.

These ideas have a well-established history in the field of organisational studies and offer a different perspective on the relationship between universities and technologies from those commonly found in educational technology. Authors such as Orlikowski, for example, have argued for some decades that technology is not some external factor that is inserted into institutions, nor is it a causal force that simply reshapes the organisations that it encounters. Instead, technology is highly political, incorporating specific interpretive schemes, functionality and organisationally sanctioned norms, and favouring the interests of some groups over others (Orlikowski 1992). As such, technology embodies politically motivated structures – but instead of assuming that these are then imposed upon people working within an organisation, Orlikowski's focus on practices reveals how technologies are appropriated by users, being taken up in ways that might support or subvert their intended uses (Orlikowski 2000). This analysis, which draws on ANT, draws attention back to the materiality of organisational life, revealing 'the absence of any considered treatment or theorizing of the material artefacts, bodies, arrangements, and infrastructures through which practices are performed' (Orlikowski 2007:1436).

These material arrangements have already been shown to be central to the ways in which students engage, as illustrated in Chapter 8 through discussion of students' efforts to create suitable study spaces. These assemblages involved arrangements of mobile and fixed materials, whether these were books being arranged in a library space, the use of the course's virtual learning environment, or the failed negotiations with others waiting to use the same networked printer. Parallel developments took place around the project described in this book, creating relationships between it and the host institution in ways that affected both – a mutual kind of 'impact'.

The Mandate for Impact

The project referred to in this book was influenced by research in the field of educational technology of the kind outlined above. As indicated in Chapter 5, the funder, JISC, recognised that organisational change was challenging, and were determined that the projects they had funded within this programme should work purposefully towards systemic, sustainable change. Their commitment to improving educational practice across the sector had contributed to their decision to commission these as development projects, not primarily as research; all the projects were expected to intervene in established practices, and provide evidence that they had improved these.

In particular, the programme had been shaped by an evaluation report, commissioned from Glenaffric Ltd but unfortunately no longer available in the public domain, which stated:

> One of the most persistent and pervasive concerns expressed about the support for the implementation of the strategy is the lack of evidence of the successful implementation of technology developments in institutions in any meaningful and scalable way. JISC initiatives continue to engage a relatively small number of enthusiasts and developers in a (growing but still limited) number of institutions, but are rarely adopted on an institutional scale. There is a particular concern about a growing imbalance between funding for technological development on the one hand, and implementation, consolidation and changing practice on the other.
>
> *(Glenaffric 2008)*

The kinds of academic staff development initiative which we will describe in Chapter 11 formed part of the response to this situation, seeking to create opportunities for individuals and groups to reflect upon and potentially develop their practice. However, another aspect of this work involved effecting change at the level of institutional policies or structures. From the perspective of work within educational technology, this might look like an issue that could be addressed through rational and instrumental means, for example, through managerial processes of setting a strategic direction and monitoring progress towards it. However, Orlikowski's analysis suggests that this account overlooks the politics of the situation and the ways in which individuals might have competing interests or might subvert the intended uses of technologies. This posed the challenge of trying to explain how an externally funded project, with only temporary legitimacy within the organisation, could influence vested interests in constructive ways.

Theorising Influence: Realities, Facts and Care

Mol's ethnographic study of the disease atherosclerosis in a Dutch hospital (Mol 2002) led to the development of *praxiology* – the study of practices. Of central importance in praxiology is the idea that the kinds of claims that doctors and patients might make about atherosclerosis did not refer in some decontextualised way to some platonic ideal of the disease, but instead reflected the specific practices of knowing the body that each actor performed – whether these involved walking, pain, interviews or the measurement of the thickening of the intima in cross-sectional tissue samples from legs, as seen under a microscope. Their claims were not claims about atherosclerosis *per se*, but about actors' relationships to it, including their ways of knowing it.

> In the traditional ordering of disciplines, an ethnographer talking about disease transgresses the thresholds separating the layers of reality in the pyramid of objects. But the move made here is different. It is not a matter of turning the arrow round so that instead of the natural sciences explaining social phenomena a social explanation of molecules, cells, or bodies is being presented. Instead, another praxis has been introduced, another approach taken: that of practice. The latter encompasses molecules and money, cells and worries, bodies, knives, and smiles, and talks about all of these in a single breath. [. . .] If practice becomes our entrance into the world, ontology is no longer a monist whole. Ontology-in-practice is multiple.
>
> *(Mol 2002:157)*

This creation of multiple 'realities' gives rise to a situation in which different versions of the world need to co-exist – and some of them do this more successfully than others. Where realities co-ordinate, Mol describes how the differences between them can be *bracketed*, allowing them to be treated as equivalent – at least until some inconsistency arises, at which point it may prove necessary to 'unbracket' them again in order to try to explain what happened (64). This process of bracketing, unbracketing and co-ordinating forms part of what Mol calls ontological politics, or a 'politics of what', which involves different actors competing in order to see whose version of reality will 'win'.

This idea of different realities being pitted against each other in contests of strength has been developed by Latour (2004) in the form of matters of concern. He notes that 'facts' have always been produced by motivated individuals, using specific instruments and within politicised settings (Latour and Woolgar 1979). The ontological politics Mol describes illustrate Latour's point, described in Chapter 9, that 'facts should be presented as 'matters of concern', making sure that the practices that produce and sustain them remain visible' (Latour 2005). Doing so allows the basis for any claim made to be interrogated and critiqued, allowing the relative strengths of competing facts to be weighed.

This also draws reflexive attention to the role of researchers. In studying any situation, researchers create new connections and relations, bringing together facts that were previously separate as they generate new accounts of things. This process of connection and juxtaposition means that researchers cannot help but add strength to some matters of concern while testing the strength of others. In other words, research will inevitably interfere in existing ontological politics, and cannot help but affect the people and things that are studied. Instead of being framed in some simplistic way as a one-directional 'impact', however, this interference may be better understood as the creation of new entanglements between assemblages. Building on this notion of ontological politics, de la Bellacasa notes:

> This discussion raises the issue of how 'we' are contributing the construction of the world. How does respect for concerns in the things we re-present encourage attention to the effects of our accounts on the composition of things?
>
> *(de la Bellacasa 2011:89)*

She goes on to develop the notion of *matters of care*, foregrounding the politics of researchers' involvement in strengthening some facts at the expense of others, and inviting direct scrutiny of the 'ethically and politically charged *practice*' (*ibid*. 90) of research. Since researchers cannot research social situations without affecting them – in other words, since they cannot help but have some kind of impact on the things that their work entangles them with – they should, she argues, make their commitments and attachments clear. Moreover, they should consider how their work affects all those who care about the object of study, whether they stand in support of it or are opposed to it.

Entanglements with the Institution

Viewed from the perspective of matters of concern, the project's work involved entangling facts about students' lives and the ongoing enactment of the institution they were registered with. Many of these were easy to bring together, supporting and reinforcing each other. For example, Nahid's use of the library and Yuki's analysis of feeling less 'bound' by place (Chapter 8) add support to established services by connecting them with positive accounts about these two students' lives. These were seen as vindicating developments that had led to the provision of digital resources, and confirming the suitability of existing library arrangements as a place for students to study. Such entanglements met little resistance; they were normally welcomed.

Some entanglements, however, did not fit so well with the existing realities of the institution. As described in Chapter 9, Juan described how his use of the library was hampered by the way printers had been set up. This stopped him from printing material double-sided and increased the costs of printing. Rather than pay for more pages, he opted to walk to another institution located a few minutes away where his girlfriend was a student. There, he would go to the library and use her institutional ID and password to log in on the other institution's network, plug a memory stick with his files on it into the desktop PC he was using, and would then print double-sided on that institution's printers. The entanglement of Juan's economic concerns with the configuration of local printers called the existing policy into question, testing the strength of comfortable beliefs about the appropriateness and value of the experience we were providing for our students.

Fortunately, the costs and issues in this case were relatively minor, and it was easy to change the facts of our printing arrangements so as to shore up the version of reality that was preferred institutionally.

Other entanglements were harder to reconcile, both institutionally and for the programme of projects as a whole. For example, the mess and complexity of students' experiences, as described in Chapters 6 to 8, called the neat progression implied in the JISC digital literacies framework into doubt. If the same student, in this case, Faith, could be seen as fluent enough to curate digital resources at one moment, but struggled to cope with printing at another, could they really be described as being 'digitally literate'? Viewing this situation as a matter of concern raised questions about the relative stability of any such classification, calling the framework's value into doubt. Viewing it as a matter of care raised questions about the politics of such a classification, what it might mean for Faith to be identified either as digitally literate or digitally illiterate, and what responsibilities the institution had towards her.

It was, however, the attempt to introduce a new IT strategy within the institution that provides the clearest example of the way in which we as researchers had to engage with matters of concern and matters of care, and which also best illustrates the way in which doing this allowed the project to effect change within the institution and achieve the kind of lasting influence on policies and structures that JISC was looking for.

This entanglement will be analysed by drawing on Law's four moments of translation, originally developed by Callon (1984) and elaborated by Fenwick, Edwards and Sawchuk (2011). This approach creates a sociomaterial analysis, drawing attention to moments when matters of concern are tested, and allowing the identification of matters of care. In this analysis, *translation* is what happens when elements come together in a network, changing one another in the process of forming links. The first 'moment' in this process is *problematisation*, when something seeks to establish itself as the defining frame for an idea or problem, and which also defines the relationship between this problem and other entities.

In this case, problematisation occurred with the development and circulation of the draft strategy. The strategy, which had been authored by the director of IT services, sought to simplify the desktop services provided to staff, reducing the amount of technical support that needed to be provided. Configurable desktop machines would be replaced by 'thin client' terminals, running a centrally specified service; this would be available across the institutional network, but not outside of the institution, reducing the need for out-of-hours support and support for non-standard technologies. This defined the problem in terms of provision of a reliable service – where reliability meant that the service operated within centrally specified parameters, resulting in fewer system failures and requiring less staff time to support. This problematisation can be characterised as being technical and economic; the social effects that might follow from the strategy were of secondary concern.

The second step, *interessement*, involves inviting entities in to support the new framing, and can also involve deliberate exclusions. In this case:

> The report [. . .] pulls together the outcomes of stakeholder and [. . .] staff meetings. The proposed programme of change has also been informed by discussions with third party organisations and advice from the UCISA IT Directors group.
>
> *(draft strategy)*

This illustrates several of the entities being 'interested' in the new strategy: stakeholders, staff, external organisations and a national professional group. The report also sought to involve students, and the category of 'staff' included academics, professional service staff and the senior management of the institution.

The next two moments are *enrolment* and *mobilisation*. Enrolment is the process through which entities become increasingly engaged in new identities and behaviours that align with the problematisation. Mobilisation then follows, describing the way in which a network that has become sufficiently stable can extend to new locations or domains. The reason that these two moments have been introduced together is because, in this case, enrolment failed; this meant that mobilisation never happened. If it had, this would have consisted of the policy, backed by various enrolled entities, extending the problematisation into new configurations of work relations, such as replacing desktop machines, phasing out existing services to introduce new ones, and leading to changes in staffing within IT services.

The problem at the moment of enrolment involved the resistance of academic staff and students. The attempt to enrol these groups rested on the promise of a more consistent and reliable service – a prospect they were expected to want. In the draft strategy, this desire was presented as a fact. Understood instead as a matter of concern, the strength of this claim to being a fact rested on records of meetings. The strength of this was soon tested when, in other meetings, academic staff spoke out about their concerns over the restrictions that would be placed on services. Students' concerns were similarly raised by representatives who were present when the draft strategy was discussed. The author of the draft countered these tests of strength against the strategy by saying that such concerns were not representative, and that the collective interest would be best served by adopting the draft. This illustrates a moment where the ontological politics of organisational life surfaced. Two versions of reality competed: one in which the director of IT services claimed to speak for the majority of staff and students, and one in which individual academics and students claimed exactly the same. There was no way to 'bracket' these inconsistencies; one or other position would have to concede and conform to the reality of the other.

The evidence produced by the project, described in the previous chapters, became entangled in this struggle. As an intervention in this trial, vignettes were constructed to illustrate the themes our analysis had identified. These vignettes described existing patterns of academic work that had proved successful. The proposal was that these vignettes could be used as 'use cases', against which the proposed strategy could be compared.

This test showed several ways in which the proposed strategy would make existing strategies for doing academic work problematic. The strategy, which focused on the experience of on-campus students, would create problems for those studying Master's courses at a distance and for the PGCE students who were off campus while on placements in schools. It might also affect campus-based students who wanted to study at other times, for example, while on public transport. Although the services as a whole would be more reliable, as measured by 'up time' of technical services being provided without interruption, they would not be as accessible. The effect of these use cases, and the consequences the strategy would have for them, reframed the question posed by the strategy. This shifted away from, 'Do we want a more reliable service?' to 'Do we want a less accessible service?'. It would still be possible to pursue the strategy, but doing so would re-categorise established study practices as inappropriate, unsupported and in many ways illegitimate. It shifted the 'obligatory passage point' that the strategy document sought to construct, away from its focus on the quality of the systems *per se*, and instead, to questions about whether the proposed system would be fit for purpose. Similar problems also arose for academic staff, many of whom worked out of hours from home, while away at conferences or during study visits to other institutions, as well as from their offices. Similarly, this led to questions about whether it was in the institution's best interests to prevent academics from working at these times.

Documenting students' experiences involved what Latour and Woolgar (1979) describe as practices of inscription, turning ephemeral, private or inaccessible experiences into material, textual and multimodal narratives that could be passed around at meetings and discussed. Bringing these experiences into the debate in this way made them visible, kept them in focus and made them harder to dismiss, because the materiality of their presence (as printed papers on a table, or as an agenda item to cover) stabilised them.

The individual academics and students who had spoken against the policy had previously been challenged as being unrepresentative. The stable presence of documented experiences added to their network of support and strengthened their claims and their version of reality. This allowed academics and students, viewed more generally as interested groups, to be enrolled behind the alternative position that was being advocated. Similarly documented experiences could not be provided for the draft strategy, in spite of reference to meetings and focus groups that had been included in the document. This left the strategy unable to enrol students and academics behind its version of reality. The potential users of the service distanced themselves from the strategy, making the proposals increasingly untenable; as a result, the strategy was abandoned.

Conclusions

Although projects might aspire to create an impact, influence is rarely one-dimensional, and richer explanations of the relationships between research, practice and policy are needed. Building such relationships is complicated and political and involves entangling assemblages that may previously have been independent of each other. The linear models of change that have historically been associated with technology adoption have failed to provide a robust account of this process. Their simplicity may be appealing, but it is not convincing.

The alternative model illustrated here explores the process through which various assemblages become entangled and the struggles for legitimacy that result. In this process, each assemblage produces a particular kind of reality; these realities develop or unravel as elements come into contact, subjecting the people and things that constitute them to tests of strength. The case that was presented here shows how projects can influence policies and practice without resorting to simplistic, heroic narratives about change, or to deterministic narratives about the inevitable impact of technology on social organisations. The outcome in this case was achieved by creating new associations, entangling the project with, and strengthening, one of the two versions of reality. The project lent support; it did not cause or decide the outcome.

However, the commitments of the project were already clearly aligned with students' experiences, understood as a matter of care. These experiences had already been cared about enough to warrant studying and documenting them; these were experiences that were valued by the students, and also by us as researchers. The experiences of students who had taken part in the project would either be protected or undermined by the proposed new strategy. It would have been inconsistent to see the developments unfolding and to have chosen not to mobilise these documents in order to support and preserve the kind of organisation, both social and material, that enabled them to happen. This, however, was not a one-way pattern of influence, but something which altered the relationship of the project with the institution, as well as altering the institution's policy. 'Impact' was distributed in various directions through this entanglement of relationships.

References

Barber, M., Donnelly, K., Rizvi, S. and Summers, L. 2013. *An Avalanche Is Coming*. London: Institute for Public Policy Research. www.ippr.org/publication/55/10432/an-avalanche-iscoming-higher-education-and-the-revolution-ahead [Accessed 10 Aug 2017].

Brown, S. 2002. Re-engineering the University. *Open Learning: The Journal of Open, Distance and e-Learning* 17(3), 231–243.

Callon, M. 1984. Some elements of a sociology of translation: domestication of the scallops and the fishermen of St Brieuc Bay. *The Sociological Review* 32(1), 196–233.

Christensen, C. 2013. *The Innovator's Dilemma: When New Technologies Cause Great Firms to Fail*. Harvard: Harvard Business Review Press.

Christensen, C. and Eyring, H. 2011. *The Innovative University: Changing the DNA of Higher Education from the Inside Out*. New York: John Wiley & Sons.

de la Bellacasa, M. 2011. Matters of care in technoscience: assembling neglected things. *Social Studies of Science* 41(1), 85–106.

Eynon, R. 2012. The challenges and possibilities of the impact agenda. *Learning, Media & Technology* 37(1), 1–3.

Fenwick, T., Edwards, R. and Sawchuk, P. 2011. *Emerging Approaches to Educational Research: Tracing the Sociomaterial*. London: Routledge.

Francis, B. 2011. Increasing impact? An analysis of the issues raised by the impact agenda in educational research. *Scottish Educational Review* 43(2), 4–16.

Geuna, A. and Martin, B. 2003. University research evaluation and funding: An international comparison. *Minerva* 41(4), 277–304.

Glenaffric. 2008. Evaluation report. No longer available in public domain.

Kennedy, E., Laurillard, D., Horan, B. and Charlton, P. 2015. Making meaningful decisions about time, workload and pedagogy in the digital age: the course resource appraisal model. *Distance Education* 36(2), 177–195.

Latour, B. 2004. Why has critique run out of steam? From matters of fact to matters of concern. *Critical Inquiry* 30(2), 225–248.

Latour, B. 2005. *Reassembling the Social: An Introduction to Actor-Network-Theory*. Oxford: Oxford University Press.

Latour, B. and Woolgar, S. 1979. *Laboratory Life: The Social Construction of Scientific Facts*. Beverly Hills: SAGE.

Laurillard, D. 2007. Modelling benefits-oriented costs for technology enhanced learning. *Higher Education* 54(1), 21–39.

Mol, A. 2002. *The Body Multiple: Ontology in Medical Practice*. Durham: Duke University Press.

Oancea, A. 2013. Interpretations of research impact in seven disciplines. *European Educational Research Journal* 12(2), 242–250.

Oliver, M. 2011. Technological determinism in educational technology research: some alternative ways of thinking about the relationship between learning and technology. *Journal of Computer Assisted Learning* 27(5), 373–384.

Orlikowski, W. 1992. The duality of technology: rethinking the concept of technology in organizations. *Organization Science* 3(3), 398–427.

Orlikowski, W. 2000. Using technology and constituting structures: a practice lens for studying technology in organizations. *Organization Science* 11(4), 404–428.

Orlikowski, W. 2007. Sociomaterial practices: exploring technology at work. *Organization Studies* 28(9), 1435–1448.

Salmon, G. 2005. Flying not flapping: a strategic framework for e-learning and pedagogical innovation in higher education institutions. *ALT-J: Research in Learning Technology* 13(3), 201–218.

Sharpe, R., Benfield, G. and Francis, R. 2006. Implementing a university e-learning strategy: levers for change within academic schools. *ALT-J: Research in Learning Technology* 14(2), 135–151.

Weller, M. 2011. *The Digital Scholar: How Technology is Transforming Scholarly Practice*. London: Bloomsbury.

11

THE ASSEMBLAGE AS LENS

Throughout this book we have argued, in a series of steps, that mainstream conceptions of student engagement in the digital university are limited in various respects, and that ultimately they distort the nature of practice. We have proposed an alternative sociomaterial model, which sees agency and practice as distributed across a range of actors, both human and nonhuman, with space and time theorised as active constituents in this process as opposed to neutral contexts. We have also explored the messy and challenging nature of entanglement in assemblages, and the ways in which 'impact' might be achieved in the context of institutional change. In this chapter, we will explore the implications of such an analysis for educational research, policy and practice.

Exploring Assemblages

In the research study, we adopted a multimodal journaling methodology as discussed in Chapter 5. The focus was on attempting to shed light on the nature of student engagement in the day-to-day practices of being a student, particularly focusing on the under-researched area of independent study in relation to the digital. In order to achieve a fine level of granularity, we used participant-generated images, videos and other forms of visual semiotic resources to shed light on their practices and perspectives. This approach was also intended to circumvent the somewhat abstracting effect of verbal account data generated through traditional semi-structured interviews, by linking the interviews to the specifics of particular devices, texts or settings, which were highlighted visually by the students. This approach is in accordance with the broader theoretical framing of the project, in that it foregrounds the agency and importance of nonhuman actors, such as devices and texts, and encourages the participants to focus on the particular and the situated, as opposed to reaching for generalisations. In this regard, it seeks to put into practice elements of the critique set out in the book – that student engagement in the digital cannot be reduced to a series of free-floating skills, attributes or types. We would suggest that the adoption of a sociomaterial understanding of engagement necessitates an ongoing qualitative and fine-grained lens on the detail of practice as it unfolds, and we would therefore advocate further in-depth 'slow' work which looks at how distributed agency and engagement plays out.

Although the previous chapter describes how the project influenced strategic plans for how technologies would be deployed in the institution, the relationship between the findings of educational research and policy remains complex, and we harbour no illusions that a small-scale study such as this, with a somewhat unconventional analysis, is likely to be picked up and applied at the level of university policy and resource allocation more broadly. However, we would argue that this study and critique forms part of a broader area of critical and practice-oriented work which challenges some of the assumptions about student engagement discussed at the start of the book.

In terms of policy, we argue that there are a series of implications which can be drawn out. The first is that student engagement spans a range of practices, which are often seen in 'teaching and learning' policy and resource allocation as separate. An example of this would be accessing digital resources and texts for reading and study – the responsibility for the development of student capacities to engage with this is conventionally seen as residing in the library, through information literacy education and support. In most UK universities, the development of academic writing, in contrast, is likely to be seen as the responsibility of an extracurricular study support unit (conventionally aimed at home or Anglophone students), or a language centre (for speakers of other languages). The use of digital devices is normally supported elsewhere, via IT support services. The ability to know how to approach a particular assignment task or how to apply research methodology is more likely to be regarded as the responsibility of the particular academic module team. The design of the physical space, infrastructure and temporal access to facilities is likely to be controlled elsewhere by senior members of professional services. There are therefore a large number of separate professional and academic teams in universities each responsible for developing and supporting different elements of student engagement, as if these elements are sequential or can be clearly separated, effectively still following a fragmented 'skills and competencies' model. This has always been problematic, but, in the context of contemporary student engagement, it appears downright anachronistic. As we have seen in the study data, all these elements of practice are intermingled, concurrent, fluid, emergent and mobile. The capacity to use devices, to make judgements about suitability of texts, to read and work critically with complex knowledge and ideas, to make notes and create texts and to engage in meaning-making and use academic conventions appropriately – all of these elements and more – cannot be meaningfully separated and developed in isolation, but co-interact in a complex web of practice and agency.

In addition, this takes place in the current UK context of sector and institutional focus on 'student satisfaction'. The complexities and extensive critiques of student satisfaction surveys and evaluations of teaching excellence are beyond the scope of this book, but a recurrent theme in the results of these exercises is the student desire for more guidance on how to approach assessment and specifically more feedback on their work. Taking this at face value, and leaving aside for a moment the related discussion of whether and to what extent providing more feedback is a sign of fostering a 'customer' relationship, we would argue that part of the ongoing challenge with this issue is agreeing the locus of responsibility for enhancing feedback and guidance to students. With time-poor academics facing increased class sizes and greater demands, the responsibility to address this issue tends to fall back on this highly fragmented, generic, extracurricular structure, which is ill-equipped to provide in-depth guidance on the specifics of particular assignments. The call to work towards a more holistic and integrated model of student development is not a new one, but we would argue that this study lends weight to the argument that the various elements of provision on offer should be redesigned, in collaboration with academic teams, to more closely reflect the nature of practice. In practical terms, this is challenging in terms of structure, funding and expertise, but it is not insurmountable. What is required is a research-informed, flexible and innovative vision at the level of senior management which is able to look beyond either the generic 'deficit' model implied by the skills agenda, or the unrealistic 'transformative' fantasies fostered by 'learning technology' enthusiasts. The following section will focus on some practical interventions which were developed as outcomes from this project, and will discuss how this type of integrated and research-informed sociomaterial approach might be scaled up and used as a lens more broadly.

Seeing Engagement Differently

One area where the findings of this particular project were applied was academic staff development and raising awareness of the nature of digital student engagement. Lyndsay Jordan, in collaboration with the UK-based Staff and Educational Development Association (SEDA), was commissioned to create a set of workshop materials to sensitise participants to a range of the findings of the project (JISC 2014). These open-access materials were developed to include six themes, plus evaluation:

1   Introducing Spaces and Places
2   Mapping Spaces and Places
3   Mapping Activities and Identities
4   Mapping Devices and Tools (1)
5   Mapping Devices and Tools (2)
6   Mapping of Texts
7   Evaluation and Next Steps

The screenshot (Figure 11.1) gives a flavour of the activities designed to be used with academics. Elements of the research data (interview transcripts plus images) were combined with reflective and discursive tasks to encourage academic staff workshop participants or individuals to reflect on their own day-to-day practices and, by extension, those of their students. The overall intention of this resource pack was to present a challenge to some of the common preconceptions about student engagement discussed throughout this book, particularly in order to shed light on what is actually required of students when they are set an assignment, with a view to providing insights about the type of support and development they might need, as shown in Figure 11.1.

This intervention is innovative in the sense that it works directly with research data and draws on it to form educational development materials and activities, as opposed to basing these on assumed general principles. It is also unusual in that it does not focus on academic staff teaching practice in the classroom or online, but instead seeks to raise awareness of student independent study practices, which are normally somewhat hidden from view. It also attempts to move away from a compartmentalising of the various elements discussed above – information literacies, the digital, study spaces, writing and so on. Instead it seeks to reveal their

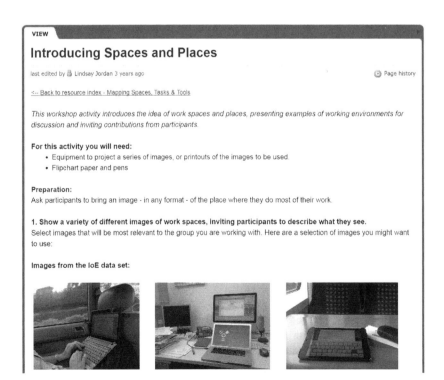

FIGURE 11.1   Introducing place and spaces screenshot from JISC

interconnected nature and poses questions about the implications for academic practice.

A further application of the findings of the project was a collaboration with library staff Nazlin Bhimani and Barbara Sakarya, who created a 'LibGuide' online resource as part of the wide set of resources available to students via the library website, again based directly on the findings of the project. The various elements of the resource can be seen in Figure 11.2 – again the data and findings were used to explore the themes arising and their implications for educational practice in the institution.

The recommendations were set out in terms of 'lessons learned'. Although these were written specifically for that institution, the implications seem potentially applicable to other institutional contexts:

1   The data support the notion that 'digital literacy' cannot be understood just in terms of individuals and skills; it needs to take into account who is doing what and where.

2   There is a need to understand digital literacies holistically, rather than focusing on any one element in isolation. On the basis of this, a project that ignores issues of access is as unlikely to be as effective as one that ignores practices or identities.

3   The discussions emphasised that digital literacy changes over time. People both learn and forget; their literacy can either be developed or lost; also, technologies develop and settings are adapted. For this reason, digital literacy should not be seen as a one-off achievement, but as something that is constantly enacted.

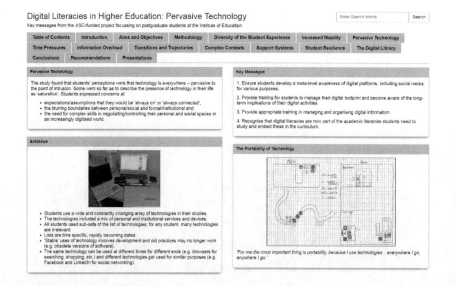

FIGURE 11.2   Pervasive technology screenshot from LibGuide

4   IOE students use a wide array of technologies for their studies including many that are not institutionally supported. These tools and services were used either because they enhanced the students' ability to act in some way or because they were required to, and were strongly intertwined with uses of 'official' IOE technologies.

5   Students had a sense that some technologies were for a specific part of their life only (study, work, entertainment) while others crossed these areas. Students differed in the extent to which they saw specific examples of this 'convergence' as desirable.

6   Many students found that the vast array of resources on and around the VLE and online library resulted in 'information overload'. In response, they developed different strategies by utilising official course guidelines and also developing individual strategies. Similar strategies had to be developed to cope with the volume of postings on VLE discussion boards.

7   Technology is seen as 'doing things' to students, not all of which are positive. In the best cases students adopt technologies in order to act more effectively or efficiently. However, technologies can also make students feel powerless or alienated, or even controlled.

8   Students sometimes opt out of technologies that they feel are controlled by the institution in order to use ones that they feel in control of instead. This included using personal email instead of the institutionally provided accounts and using Skype rather than the VLE for communication.

(*UCL IOE:2014*)

The following recommendation was also set out for the institution on the basis of the research:

> The strong degree of interaction between personal devices and institutional hardware, official and unofficial applications, institutional and non-institutional spaces, and student, private and professional identities, has implications for how the institution creates infrastructures for study. The diversity of practices that were evidence needed to be acknowledged as standard practice and actively facilitated by not only maximising the simplicity and efficiency of interfaces with institutional technologies, but also proactively supporting the use of networked mobile devices.
>
> (*UCL IOE:204*)

The emphasis here is on acknowledging the complexity and diversity of engagement, and planning for it when maintaining and creating infrastructures. Mobile networked devices are emphasised as central to practice, but institutional spaces and devices are also seen as an important part of the model – this reflected the mixed nature of student engagement as seen in the study, where students reported a range of mobile practices but also valued the stability of institutional spaces.

The study also led to a third implementation project, in which Stephen Hill at the Academic Writing Centre (AWC) took a short course previously only available as a traditional face-to-face series of classroom sessions, and offered it as an online synchronous course to a small group of students using the synchronous online teaching interface Blackboard Collaborate. The rationale for this was that, given the strongly digital nature of academic writing, it would be more congruent with contemporary student practice to offer this provision in an online setting, also recognising the geographically distributed nature of the student body both internationally and across the London area. A focus group was held afterwards in which students reported a mixed reaction. Some students felt the lack of visual co-presence rendered the interaction more difficult, and also reported that the use of online breakout groups felt isolating in comparison with group work in a classroom where the students remain co-present. However, students who were speakers of other languages reported that they found the text-based chat facility allowed them enhanced opportunities for interaction. The pros and cons of online synchronous provision versus face-to-face classes is an extensive topic which is beyond the scope of this chapter to explore in depth. However, it is worth noting that the importance of embodied co-presence came up in the student reactions to this intervention – again underscoring the point that bare functionality does not seem to be sufficient or regarded as a satisfactory way to engage with students digitally, and that the need for embodied co-presence remains a factor. In the light of this, the AWC has continued to develop online provision and to emphasise the development of online resources and the centrality of the digital to academic writing, via the development of VLE-based and open web resources such as the page shown in Figure 11.3:

However, the centre has not moved wholesale to online provision, instead deliberately adopting a hybrid model which attempts to reflect the diversity of student digital engagement with reading and writing that was found in the study. This is a deliberate and pragmatic rejection of ideologically led models which

FIGURE 11.3 AWC screenshot

would seek to replace face-to-face with online provision, through a belief in the online having superseded the analogue; instead, in response to the project findings, the material, social and embodied nature of student digital practice is recognised and cultivated.

So far, this chapter has described three small initiatives that attempted to interpret and implement the findings of the study described in the preceding chapters, across various different areas of one institution. The effects were modest, but we argue that they represent an attempt to respond to the complex and nuanced picture that we had glimpsed of student digital engagement in the study. However, the point could legitimately be raised that wider-scale developments in the sector cannot rely on small-scale and time-consuming local qualitative studies alone, but instead need to identify broader principles upon which to base their strategies and allocation of resource. This runs the risk of taking us full circle, back to the 'skills and competencies' frameworks we critiqued in Chapter 4. The remaining part of this chapter will return to this issue and will seek to address how we might move beyond frameworks in order to retain the nuances and insights of a sociomaterial sensibility, while also offering applicability beyond the immediate context.

Beyond Frameworks

As we have argued, there are two principal and persistent objections to the models that have been offered to explain student engagement. The first is the mismatch between the compartmentalised and sequential assumptions of the models in contrast with the tangled and nonlinear nature of contemporary student engagement. The second is the underscoring of humanist assumptions about practice, which persist in imbuing students with all the agency, in a fantasy that bears scant relationship to the messy, entangled, emergent, contingent networks formed with the nonhuman actors that were observed in the study. Critiquing existing frameworks or provision, however, is easier than proposing an alternative, and a legitimate response to the analysis above could be, 'so what?'. The question arises as to whether the alternative sociomaterial perspective on student engagement with the digital can (or even should) lead to a useful alternative type of perspective.

We have argued that engagement and practice is always sociomaterially situated and entangled in complex networks of actors, both human and nonhuman. We have also proposed that engagement is nonlinear, fluid and emergent, as opposed to cumulative and composed of discrete, trainable skills. However, the fact remains that students may still need guidance, awareness raising and support around digital engagement for academic work. In the remaining section of this chapter, we propose an alternative perspective, which seeks to recognise the complex nature of emergent practice while also offering a reflective (as opposed to normative) lens for academic staff and students, through which to gain insights into the types of networks they will need to engage with in order to conduct their academic studies.

One of the challenges of creating such a lens is the need to move away from hierarchical, simplified or compartmentalised visual representations, and instead attempt to represent the relational and entangled nature of practice. The preceding chapters illustrate the kinds of elements that form the assemblages needed for studying. Importantly, these elements are indicative: new elements could and should be added, to reflect the ways in which studying takes place in other contexts. As discussed in Chapter 4, there is a tendency for models and frameworks to slip from a well-grounded empirical description into a normative, categorical mode, in order to appear universal. The elements identified here are drawn from the examples used in the book; they are, therefore, indicative of things that can be important when studying. They provide a useful repertoire of the kinds of things a new lens on practice might seek to include. However, these lists could and should be developed. In each list, we also include relevant elements identified in other chapters for clarity; for example, in the list of spatial infrastructure, elements that arose in earlier chapters are included alongside those from Chapter 9. It would be perfectly possible to regroup elements if that made more sense for a particular set of local practices.

Chapter 7 explored the range of human and nonhuman elements that were involved in these assemblages. These included:

• Texts (articles, chapters, websites, surveys, notes), including multimodal texts (videos, music, images)
• Digital devices (laptops, smartphones, desktop computers, tablets, cameras, electronic whiteboards, printers)
• Digital applications (Word, Excel, PowerPoint, data analysis software, reference management software)
• Analogue devices (pens, highlighter markers, folders, Post-it notes)
• People (other students, teachers, family, friends, technical helpdesk staff, translators).

Chapter 8 focused on spaces and times, identifying a variety of elements that could be included:

• Institutional spaces (the library, lecture rooms), including social spaces (the student bar, the foyer, the lobby)
• Personal spaces (kitchens, bedrooms, parked cars)
• Public spaces (cafes, parks, buses, trains, aeroplanes)
• Times (scheduled time such as classes, personal time outside of the curriculum, 'dead' time reclaimed from boredom)
• Rhythms and paces (repetitions, schedules, intrusive notifications and reminders, intensification, breaks)

- Histories (through notebooks or texts, previous versions of software being replaced)
- Futures (deadlines).

In Chapter 9, attention was drawn to elements of infrastructure that might be important in supporting study. Many of these can be taken for granted if they work as intended; in analysis, there is always a decision to be taken about where to 'cut' the network (Latour 1999):

- Digital services, in the institution (login ID, the library's digital collection, the virtual learning environment, email) and beyond (Google, Google Scholar, other email services, Twitter, Skype, cloud storage)
- The institution's physical infrastructure (Wi-Fi, desks, chairs) and potentially the broader physical infrastructure (public Wi-Fi, benches, roads, the cables that form the internet)
- Personal infrastructure (beds, baths, tables, home Wi-Fi).

Study Networks

A potential move beyond frameworks would be to use a series of prompts, such as the elements listed above, as a heuristic in order to focus participants on the sociomaterial components likely to intermingle for a particular task or purpose. We have used this approach extensively in workshop mode with academic staff and students, showing visual examples from the study, and then asking participants to create and then reflect on and discuss their own drawings, maps or diagrams of practice, using the same approach. This has proved effective in revealing and providing depth on existing practices, and we have also used it to encourage participants to plan ahead for future work or, in the case of academic staff, to envisage the detail of situated, sociomaterial student engagement in their assignments and independent study. In this regard, this has proved successful as a sociomaterial lens on student engagement which can be used by students and staff, in interactive contexts, or equally for individual reflection. An online reflective resource or an app could be developed using a combination of visual elements and prompt questions to allow participants to reflect on and represent what might be labelled in more everyday terms their own evolving and changing 'Study Networks'. This resource could be used as a heuristic to raise student awareness of the complexities of study tasks and activities, combining digital and analogue elements, what they will need, and when they might seek support and guidance if required. This type of resource may also be used to support independent study, by focusing on planning and scheduling for students undertaking an assignment, asking them to think in specific material and situated terms about the detail of how they will approach the task, what will be required, how long it will take and so on. A resource such as this could be used throughout a module, in class or online, to provide some scaffolding to students as they progress their independent work, and it could also be used by academic staff as a dialogic resource to flag up student developmental needs around independent study. It could also form part of the resource used by study support units, writing centres, language centres, libraries and student-facing IT training providers, attempting to bridge across these services with an institution-wide lens. Figure 11.4 shows a detail taken from a larger diagram, created by Django in the study, which illustrates the type of image plus accompanying note which might be generated with such a resource. It is shown in its entirety in Figure 11.4 and broken down into sections in Figures 11.5–11.8.

Arguably, a similar ethos could be adopted as part of planning and resource allocation processes at an institutional level, in which decision-makers could be encouraged (perhaps through a related series of question prompts and building floor plans) to consider in a more integrated and holistic manner the specifics of how, where and when students might engage with the digital on campus and beyond – creating the conditions for the sort of insight and challenge to strategy and planning discussed in the previous chapter. Ideally, this could be supported by regular

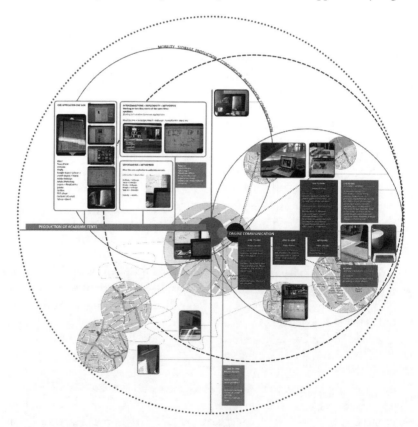

FIGURE 11.4 Django's diagram

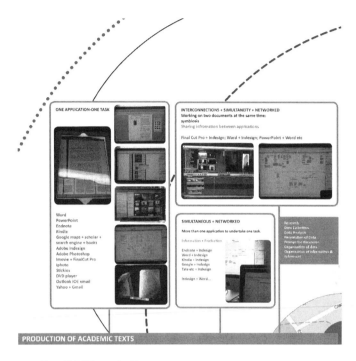

FIGURE 11.5 Detail 1 Django's diagram

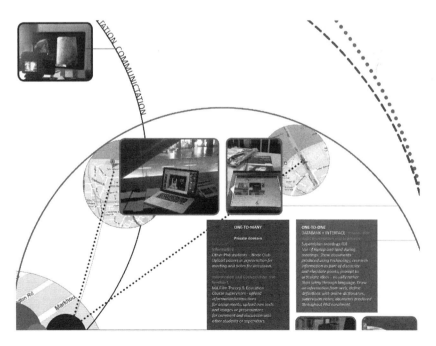

FIGURE 11.6 Detail 2 Django's diagram

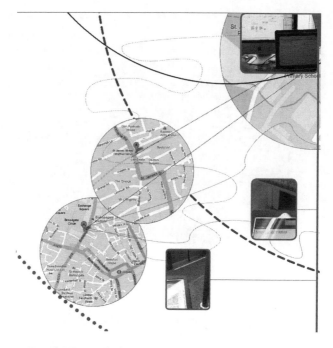

FIGURE 11.7 Detail 3 Django's diagram

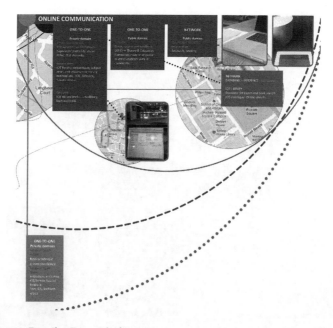

FIGURE 11.8 Detail 4 Django's diagram

qualitative small-scale institutional research studies in order to keep in touch with the reality of student digital engagement. This could also be supported by an emphasis on student input into decision-making, maintaining this practice-based focus. This perspective could serve to anchor decisions regarding space and infrastructure in the granularity of day-to-day unfolding practice, as opposed to drawing on somewhat abstract and even ideological notions of what student engagement 'ought' to be.

References

JISC. 2014. *Quick Guide: Developing Students' Digital Literacy*. Bristol: JISC. https:// digitalcapability.jiscinvolve.org/wp/files/2014/09/JISC_REPORT_Digital_Literacies_ 280714_PRINT.pdf [Accessed 10 Aug 2017].

Latour, B. 1999. On recalling ANT. *The Sociological Review* 47(1), 15–25.

UCL. 2014. 'LibGuide'. Internal online resource. UCL Institute of Education.

12
CONCLUSIONS

Throughout this book, we have sought to examine aspects of how practices involving the digital have been framed and conceptualised in the research literature and in policy and educational development. We have critiqued assumed binaries separating the digital and the analogue and also the categories and typologies applied to students. We argued for a reinstatement of the centrality of texts (of all types) to our conception of digital literacies and proposed an alternative analysis of student practices. What unites these ideas is a move away from abstract and ideological conceptions, and towards situating digital literacies in various ways as entangled in the complex 'mess' of unfolding day-to-day practice. We took a further step in 'resituating' digital literacies but bringing the focus back to the embodied nature of all digital engagement, and also a step further by arguing that time and space – conventionally seen as aspects of 'context' – themselves form an agentive part of networks of practice. We then introduced resilience as a key concept which can help us to theorise and understand the complexities and struggles surrounding entangling with assemblages in the digital university, drawing on sociomaterial perspectives. We explored an alternative model of 'impact' and change in institutions, and proposed a sociomaterial lens as a heuristic on practice as a means of moving away from the assumptions of frameworks.

Throughout this work, we have returned repeatedly to a series of central ideas: about students' engagement and experience; about the digital; about abstract models; and about what might count as evidence in relation to these things. To draw these together, each of these central ideas will be reviewed briefly here.

Engagement and Experience

Contemporary policy in Higher Education has been shaped by two inconsistent sets of discourses about students, as discussed in Chapter 1. The idea of 'the student experience' – often presented as if it were singular and homogeneous – has formed the basis for a set of market-driven, student-as-customer policies, associated with a passive view of the student-as-consumer. Meanwhile, 'learning and teaching' policies have focused on the idea of student engagement associated with observable interactions between students and with academics. Through the discussion of these ideas and the examples provided in the empirical section of this book, both sets of discourses have been shown to be ideologically driven and overly abstract. Even discussions of obviously material concerns, such as the design of learning spaces, have carried this ideological quality.

By contrast, the sociomaterial analysis of students' day-to-day study practices has revealed the importance of practices such as reading, writing and even simply thinking. These may not be visible, particularly within the formal curriculum, but they are nevertheless a central part of students' experiences. This analysis stands as a critique of the idea of active engagement and offers the possibility that we may be able to reclaim the value of unobserved, private study. In particular, a sociomaterial perspective helps to avoid naïve student-centrism by decentring the individual in the analysis. Rather than the free-floating, neoliberal subject suggested by these policy discourses, a sociomaterial perspective resituates discussions of engagement within practices. New Literacy Studies began this move by drawing attention to the way in which practices were situated within disciplines; and Actor-Network Theory has allowed this process to continue, re-tethering students' practices to specific spaces and times and to particular human and nonhuman actors. This move has allowed us to re-think agency in the digital university. Unlike the fixed positions of either the student experience or student engagement discourses, students are not universally either passive consumers nor active creators; instead, their agency is mediated by the networks of human and nonhuman actors in which they are entangled, and agency is distributed across the elements of these networks in complex and shifting ways.

Rethinking the Digital

Just as discourses about students have taken inconsistent positions, discussions about technology have similarly created a series of unhelpful binaries. Deterministic discourses have suggested the inevitable transformation of practice as an effect of the digital. Alongside this, technologies have been presented as passive, standing ready to be used as tools by agential users. The analysis has shown that both positions are oversimplifications. Just as students' agency was not an essential feature but an emergent quality of the networks with which they were entangled, so too with technology.

This dynamic returned in the discussion of impact and entanglement, showing that institutions, just like students, are neither purely users of technology nor entirely powerless before it. While contemporary discussions within educational technology may promise 'revolutions', what marked the experiences that students described, and the analysis of policy development, were continuities. Existing entanglements may well change and adapt, but they are very hard to dismiss – particularly those knitted together through stable, material connections such as an institutional infrastructure, or through well-established and widespread practices such as reading and note taking.

Accompanying both of these discourses, 'digital dualisms' have sought to draw clear divisions between the face-to-face and 'e-learning' and between ideas of embodiment and 'being online'. The analysis of materiality and embodiment questioned this separation and particularly the assumed immateriality of virtual or digital things. Instead, the ongoing persistence of what Hayles has described as 'embodied virtuality' (Hayles 1999) was visible across the accounts of our students. The digital was re-materialised in the devices, texts and infrastructure they worked with, even as it was presented on screens. These existed alongside, and were entwined with, analogue practices such as reading and writing. Paying close attention to the minutiae of emergent practices revealed how the fantasies of a digital revolution simply overlooked the rich, developing and creative way in which material things continue to matter in the digital university.

After Models

The temptation of frameworks and models, which appear to transcend specific examples and provide universal guidance, was explored. Rather than transcending day-to-day experiences, however, such abstractions run the risk of lapsing into what Leander and Lovvorn (2006) refer to as naïve formalism. Close examination of students' day-to-day practices reveals the ways in which such models over-simplify the practices they were derived from. Because of this, while they might suggest or inspire, they should always be treated with caution, with a hint of scepticism about the strength of their foundations so that they remain as matters of concern, rather than seeming to be matters of fact (Latour 2005).

However, there remains a need across the sector for the insights of research into student engagement with the digital and its relationship to practice to be understood, without relying on small-scale and localised research projects alone. We have argued that the apparently relevant models and frameworks should be treated with caution, and that (however well intentioned) the cumulative, skills-based and apparently 'closed' nature of mainstream educational frameworks relating to student digital engagement may in fact reinforce misleading oversimplifications about the nature of practice and emphasise ideologically driven stereotypes about students, academics, knowledge, meaning-making, the digital and ultimately the university itself. Our proposal is to move towards a more exploratory stance and lens on student engagement, one which is divergent rather than convergent, knowingly incomplete, messy and contingent – like practice itself.

This lens seeks to be a reflection on the day-to-day practices of the participants in this project, one designed to allow for agencies other than the student. Importantly, it contains areas that can remain blank, ready to be filled out by whoever engages with it so that it can reflect local practices. The warrant for its design consists of the analysis throughout the earlier chapters of the book. It is an invitation to others to engage in the kinds of analysis of students' study practices that we have undertaken here, so that new entanglements can be made between other students' practices, other institutions' policies and the work of the project.

Methodologies, Theory and Possible Next Steps

Given the rapid changes taking place with technology, snapshot studies of practice can date very quickly. Because of this, our approach involved following students over a period of time to understand how practices move, how effects emerge from networks and what work has to be done to sustain them. This enabled the analysis to explain the fluidity of practices, rather than purely describing an historical moment. Taken together, the approach adopted here has enabled us to understand student engagement in new ways, exploring the ongoing developments of practice in ways that are situated socially and materially, without lapsing into the simplistic position of treating either humans or technology as the sole motivating force behind the movements we observed, or lapsing into cliché and abstraction.

We have drawn on the methodological work of Actor-Network Theory and of researchers pursuing sociomaterial analyses of practice. If we had treated either students or technology as the sole source of agency, as is commonplace in Higher Education and educational technology research, we could have relied on experimental designs to understand cause and effect. Instead, to understand how agency plays out across complex entanglements, and to avoid decontextualised abstractions, it was important to adopt an approach that could explain how network effects emerged. This required close description of practice and a fine-grained approach that could follow the actors, human and nonhuman, to understand how they moved between assemblages, and what happened when they did. The theoretical work of decentring the human made it important that individuals were not the unit of analysis in this work. Instead, examples of practice – understood as complex, networked and fluid – became the focus.

Fluid Research

Like any other complex assemblage, this research study is a messy, contingent and necessarily unfinished entity. This book as a document, and eventual material artefact, may give some fleeing impression of completion, but this is as much of an illusion as the tidy nature of the frameworks and apparent fixities we have sought to destabilise. It may be that the work of this book is sufficient to allow others to incorporate these perspectives into the assemblages of their own work, but, like any fluid assemblage, the new configurations that may result are impossible to predict. Inevitably, though, as emergent digital practices and new theoretical insights continue to emerge and intertwine, new perspectives will be added to this endlessly complex, shifting and fascinating area of educational and social practice. The insights of posthuman theory and new materialist perspectives continue to present insistent and fundamental questions, blurring apparent common-sense delineations and asking us again and again to question our assumptions about agency, knowledge, technology and the human. The challenge, we argue, is for educationalists to allow space for these questions to be heard and in doing so, allow for always-unfolding, nuanced understandings of the digital, student engagement and ultimately Higher Education itself.

References

Hayles, N. K. 1999. *How We Became Posthuman*. London: University of Chicago Press.

Latour, B. 2005. *Reassembling the Social: An Introduction to Actor-Network-Theory*. Oxford: Oxford University Press.

Leander, K. and Lovvorn, J. 2006. Literacy networks: following the circulation of texts, bodies and objects in the schooling and online gaming of one youth. *Cognition and Instruction* 24(3), 291–340.

INDEX